THE PLEASURE OF READING

THE PLEASURE OF READING

Novels
and their
Writers and Readers

ERIC MACFARLANE

Matador
9 Priory Business Park,
Wistow Road, Kibworth Beauchamp,
Leicestershire. LE8 0RX
Tel: 0116 279 2299
Email: books@troubador.co.uk
Web: www.troubador.co.uk/matador
Twitter: @matadorbooks

ISBN 978 1838590 192

British Library Cataloguing in Publication Data.
A catalogue record for this book is available from the British Library.

Printed and bound in Great Britain by 4edge Limited
Typeset in 11pt Ten Oldstyle by Troubador Publishing Ltd, Leicester, UK

Matador is an imprint of Troubador Publishing Ltd

For readers everywhere

Contents

About the Author

Eric Macfarlane has worked as a teacher, head-teacher, college principal, education officer and trainer of university staff. He is an established author known particularly for his championing of creative, practical and out-of-school learning experiences. He is totally committed to an educational system that recognises children as individuals, each with particular interests, strengths and aspirations to be developed. He believes that everyone has the potential to lead a full and rewarding life, if they can find activities that absorb them and people with whom they can share them. One of his own interests is the reading of fiction - both contemporary novels and those that have stood the test of time. His new book shares the pleasure that he derives from reading and discussing books.

Introduction

The last time my wife and I moved house we spent an inordinate amount of time trying to downsize, without moving too far from the area in which we had brought up our family. Our prolonged search took us into numerous homes, which provided an interesting insight into other people's lives. The revelation that surprised me most was the number of houses we viewed that appeared to be completely devoid of books: either there weren't any, or they had been hidden away in the tidying-up process prior to our visit. Or possibly they'd all been dumped, considered superfluous with the advent of E-books.

Whatever the explanation of this bookless landscape, it made me realise just how important books are to me and how much of my time they occupy – not just reading and re-reading them, but collecting and handling them, comparing and discussing titles and authors, sharing my responses to my reading with others, recording especially noteworthy moments, thumbing through pages in search of a half-remembered passage, sorting through the crowded shelves for an old novel, or trying to find space for a new one. And, of course, browsing in bookshops and choosing gifts for friends and relations. It would create an enormous void in my life if these pleasurable activities were suddenly denied me, and I realise how fortunate I've been in having encountered a number of circumstances that conspired to save me from this fate.

It was this realisation that prompted me to take a break from my usual preoccupation with the state of education in this country and engage in a period reflecting on the pleasures of reading fiction and the authors that I've particularly enjoyed. If this seems somewhat self-indulgent, let me quickly add that I hope my observations on the writing and reading processes will be of interest to like-minded readers and serve as a stimulus for both informal discussion and for the thousands of reading and book groups that meet regularly up and down the country. Many of the books that I mention will be known to readers; others will perhaps find their way onto 'must read' lists. I hope, too, that what I have to say will be helpful to students and teachers of literature, not least because it addresses the reasons why so many young people are put off reading fiction by their English literature exam courses at school. You don't have to be a student of literature in order to enjoy reading. But, equally, academic study and reading for pleasure shouldn't be mutually exclusive.

This is a personal record of some of the books I've read and my reaction to them, told against the background of my family life and my career as an educationist. In the process of compiling it I've come to appreciate the truth that lies at the heart of fiction.

1.

The Digger Gnome and Other Childhood Reading Experiences

I was brought up in a small family – just my grandmother, unmarried mother and myself. My mother worked as a book-keeper, was always smartly dressed, and maintained an air of middle-class respectability at odds with the lifestyles of the various manual workers and their families who were our neighbours. The most bizarre feature of this class-consciousness was that in my early childhood I was privately educated, at one of the last surviving Dame Schools, run by an unqualified elderly spinster. This educational establishment, known simply as Miss Falkner's, catered for some eight or nine boys and girls, aged from five to fourteen, who spent each day grouped round a large table in the poky front room of the teacher's modest little house. The congestion in this classroom, which housed a piano and all the rest of the school's resources, would have rendered a modern health and safety inspector speechless.

At the end of each school year every pupil at Miss Falkner's received a book prize as 'a reward for general progress'. My first prize, and first ever book, was *The Digger Gnome Earns a Pippity Pebble.* Upon looking up this volume the other day, I was surprised to discover that one of the characters, whom I had remembered as the Kinky Witch, was in fact known as the Kinksy Witch. Strange what tricks the memory plays.

My Digger Gnome narrative was a slight work but, as I passed through the various stages of my education at Miss Falkner's, I acquired further confirmation of my progress in the form of more weighty tomes, most notably R.M.Ballantyne's *The Young Fur Traders,* James Fenimore Cooper's *The Last of the Mohicans* and Daniel Defoe's *Robinson Crusoe.* I enjoyed the illustrations in these books, but the task of reading the text was beyond me. Many years later, when studying for an honours degree in English, I did succeed in ploughing through *Robinson Crusoe,* which was one of our prescribed texts. It was a turgid experience that made me feel a little better about my lack of enthusiasm for the novels that I received as prizes at Miss Falkner's.

I also read Defoe's *Journal of the Plague Year* at university, an altogether more interesting, lively and succinct narrative. This lesser-known Defoe work purports to be a personal account of one Londoner's recollections of the Great Plague in 1665-6 which claimed so many citizens' lives. The book records events in great detail, naming actual neighbourhoods, streets and even houses. The narrator's first-hand descriptions and the accounts that he receives from people whom he meets all give the impression that the author was actually there. But Defoe was only 5-6 years old in 1665-6. The verisimilitude is achieved by meticulous research, in the same way that a number of modern novelists, with no direct experience of either of the two world wars, have managed to convey the horrors and bravery of the battlefields with the immediacy of an eye-witness.

It was some fifty years later that I read Defoe's *Moll Flanders,* which brings together a number of well-established narrative traditions and fuses them into what is often regarded as one of the forerunners of the modern novel. Claims of that kind depend, of course, on how you define the term 'novel'; but there is no denying that Defoe was ahead of his time in getting inside a character and bringing her vividly to life. *Moll Flanders* is a wickedly entertaining account of a professional shoplifter, pickpocket and robber who takes great delight in telling her story of dissembling and law-breaking.

We had only a few books in our home when I was young. I remember, in particular, a battered old encyclopaedia, a collection of spooky Welsh fairy stories and a book of furniture designs that had belonged to my grandfather, who had worked for a High Wycombe chair firm. There might also have been a dictionary, but I can't be certain of that. This collection grew over the years, partly by virtue of my Falkner progress prizes but also as a consequence of Christmas presents given to me by my mother and grandmother.

Throughout the year our small family lived very frugally, but Christmas was a time of relative indulgence. It was not that we exchanged large numbers of presents or consumed vast quantities of food, but there were certain small seasonal luxuries purchased that never varied from year to year – a drum of Turkish delight, a box of sweet biscuits decorated with small figures made of icing, and, when my mother worked in London, a superior packet of ground coffee bought from a smart shop in South Molton Street in Mayfair. These items were purchased well in advance of Christmas and taken out numerous times before the festivities, to be examined and admired.

Another Christmas extravagance was that I would always be presented with a hardback book, signed by either my mother or grandmother. This was during the war years and the quality and price of books reflected the shortage of paper at that time. I have retained one example – an adventure story called *Guy For Trouble* by Vivian Butler. The flyleaf contains the inscription 'War Time Production and Costs (6/-).' The coarse paper is a dirty grey and the print extremely small, with minimal space between the lines. The reader is, however, assured by the publisher that the book 'is easy to handle, completely legible, takes up less space on your bookshelf, is cheaper to post, and withal is full pre-war length and value'.

Despite the problems of war-time publishing, some good quality books continued to be produced and it was from these that my Christmas presents were generally selected. My mother made the purchases and no doubt paid the price for her desire for some signs of luxury to attend our Christmas celebrations. Moreover, although she was too busy and cash-strapped to indulge her latent interest in literature on her own behalf, she chose my presents very carefully and was manifestly much better than Miss Falkner in assessing what might be appropriate for me at a particular age. I still have some of these expensive-looking items of memorabilia from my mid-childhood and early teenage years – Arthur Ransome's *The Picts and the Martyrs*, Hilda Lewis's fantasy *The Ship That Flew,* and 'a medley of prose and verse' entitled *No 12A Joy Street.*

These Christmas presents were moments of moderate culture in my otherwise pedestrian reading habits. Depending on your view of comics, it was fortuitous or unfortunate that the 1930s saw the advent of the immensely popular *Beano* and *Dandy* strip cartoons, for at eight or nine I became keenly interested in the antics of their leading characters – Desperate Dan (the cow-pie eating cowboy), Dennis the Menace, Keyhole Kate and, of course, my near-namesake, Spanky Mcfarland. The *Beano* and *Dandy* were outrageously politically-incorrect publications, featuring a range of characters whose obesity, spottiness, lack of intelligence and other deficiencies were regarded as appropriate objects of ridicule.

These comics were shared among my friends and contemporaries and they were pretty grubby by the time my turn came round. However, in my teenage years I was able to buy my own reading material. From an early age I had a standard five-bob-a-week paper round, but at a later stage I became a really big earner, receiving the astronomical sum of twelve shillings and sixpence for a huge seven-day-a-week delivery task that also included collecting the money from householders every Saturday morning.

Some of this income went straight back to the newsagent to fund my reading. By this time I had moved on to the boys' adventure papers that had become almost an obsession with the 'working class'. My favourites were the *Adventure*, *Wizard*, *Hotspur* and *Rover*, all published by D.C.Thompson & Co. Although each paper had its particular emphasis and favourite characters, their diet was much the same – short, exciting stories of supermen, robots, death-defying pilots and commandos, amazing athletes, pugilists and soccer stars – invariably centre-forwards who couldn't stop scoring.

School stories also featured, but these were really the stock-in-trade of another group of adventure papers – *Champion*,

Magnet, *Gem* and the girls' story paper, *Girls' Crystal*. Whereas the Thompson papers often featured working class heroes, this second group focused unashamedly on the traditional public school, a world unattainable but nonetheless attractive to its readership. I regularly bought copies of all these publications, including the *Girls' Crystal*, which I found mildly titillating. I particularly liked the *Magnet* with its Frank Richards' stories of Billy Bunter, 'the Owl of the Remove'. Later on, a new paper, forged from a merger of the *Magnet* and *Gem*, contained stories featuring Sexton Blake, a poor man's Sherlock Holmes; these, too, became a favourite series.

My own experience as a teenager was inevitably mundane in comparison to the exciting lives of the fictitious heroes in my comics. Yet it was not without its adventures. My grandmother, who was mainly responsible for my upbringing, allowed me considerable freedom, and my mother, when she took charge, was more likely to ask me why I wasn't 'out in the fresh air' than to make the more customary parental enquiry about the completion of homework. This attitude didn't square very well with her decision to send me to a private school for my early education, but then that, I'm sure, had more to do with keeping up our middle class pretensions than a concern for my scholastic progress. Certainly, once I'd won a free place to the grammar school, she never put me under pressure to distinguish myself academically.

The consequence of this laissez-faire approach to parenthood was that for much of the time I ran wild, spending hours away from home. I roamed far and wide, both on my own and with the village riff-raff, whose gang I ultimately commanded. We fought with rival groups from other villages, occasionally in close combat with sticks, but more often at a distance with stones, either thrown or lethally propelled by catapult.

The Buckinghamshire road in which I lived was bounded by farmland on one side and a large country estate owned by the gentleman racing driver, Earl Howe, on the other. We used both areas of private land quite freely, making camps in farmers' haystacks, helping ourselves to plums, apples and cherries from the many Chiltern orchards, and setting our snares to catch Earl Howe's rabbits. Such activities did not of course go entirely unnoticed by the landowners and we had some scary encounters. I still have a long scar on the inside of my left leg inflicted whilst scrambling over a barbed wire fence with my companions, hotly pursued by a bull-like farmer called Brant whose stick we knew would be applied liberally to our backsides if he caught us. One day a group of us broke into the gamekeepers' shed where Earl Howe's men kept all their equipment, only to be interrupted by a posse of gamekeepers, one of whom let fly with his double-barrelled shotgun as we fled. He was probably shooting over our heads, but we didn't raise that possibility when we recounted the adventure to our contemporaries.

I led a dual life in the 1940's. Alongside my uninhibited lifestyle at weekends and in holidays, I followed a quite different routine at the Royal Grammar School High Wycombe, a highly respectable, regimented and academically-rigorous educational establishment much concerned with grooming 'high fliers' for Oxbridge. Potential scholars were identified early, classified as either linguists or scientists and given intensive preparation for the entrance exams set by the country's two most prestigious universities. The rest of us, referred to by some of the masters as 'the pits', followed a more general course designated 'Modern', a name later applied to the post-war secondary schools established for those who failed the 11+.

Although this new environment was a considerable culture shock, I adapted, as children do, toed the line and kept out of trouble – most of the time. I was happy enough and learnt to take what I could from the system. But I never saw the relevance of much of what we did. My subsequent opposition to the grammar school concept owes a good deal to my eight years as a pupil at one of its most prestigious manifestations. Schools that select on a basis of children's academic potential invariably become over-concerned with knowledge acquisition, formal methods of teaching and testing, early specialisation and intensive grooming for traditional academic universities. The result is that their students miss out on many other educational experiences they need in order to lead fulfilled lives and to function effectively in the outside world.

Good schools seek to inculcate a love of learning and one of the greatest gifts they can give their young students, as part of that process, is the habit of reading for pleasure. The academics who devised the syllabuses for the RGS, and the begowned masters who talked their way through them, were clearly oblivious of such aspirations. My early grammar school encounters with literature included the study of R.L.Stevenson's *Travels with a Donkey*, John Stewart Mill's *On Liberty*, Sir Thomas More's *Utopia* and Addison and Steele's *Coverley Papers*. They didn't feature among the experiences that I found enjoyable as a teenager. I think I must have switched off completely in English literature lessons because, apart from one notable exception, I cannot think of anything that we read other than the four titles I've already mentioned. There must have been many more, but I simply can't dredge them up from my memory.

The one spectacular exception to this barren literary landscape was our set text for the School Certificate exam, Hardy's *Mayor of Casterbridge,* a novel that held my attention from the moment I read the first spine-tingling chapter. I can still remember the low-key opening sentence that contains no hint of the drama to come:

> "One evening of late summer, before the nineteenth century had reached one-third of its span, a young man and woman, the latter carrying a child, were approaching the large village of Weydon-Priors, in Upper Wessex, on foot."

Hardy gives us a detailed picture of the man – his demeanour, the way he's dressed and hints of his occupation and character. He's a 'fine figure, swarthy and stern in aspect'. 'His measured, springless walk' is that of 'the skilled countryman as distinct from the desultory shamble of the general labourer'; while in the way he turns and plants each foot there's a hint of a 'dogged and cynical indifference, personal to himself'. The description of the woman concentrates on her face – mobile and attractive, but occasionally overlaid by a hard and half-apathetic expression that suggests someone 'who deems anything possible at the hands of Time and Chance, except perhaps fair play'.

The family meet a turnip hoer whom the husband engages in conversation. We learn from this exchange that the husband is a hay-trusser looking for work and accommodation. The turnip-hoer is pessimistic about the prospect of the travellers' finding either work or accommodation in Weydon-Priors.

The husband's manner and response give us further insights into his character and mood.

It's been Country Fair Day in Weydon-Priors and the family enter the field on the outskirts of the village looking for something to eat and drink. The day is nearing a close and the day's business of buying and selling is almost over. The refreshment booths are, however, still open.

The wife steers her husband away from the prominent beer tent, the significance of which action soon becomes clear. They enter a smaller booth specialising in furmity, a concoction of corn, flour, milk and dried fruit. The husband, 'with the instinct of a perverse character', quickly senses that there's more going on in the furmity tent than it appears at first sight and he duly passes his bowl up for it to be laced with rum. His wife sadly perceives that in steering her husband 'off the rocks of the licensed liquor-tent she had only got into maelstrom depths here amongst the smugglers'.

Having finished her furmity, the wife reminds her husband that they have to find shelter for the night and need to be on their way. He, however, is settling down for an evening's drinking and asks for further bowls of furmity, laced with increasingly large quantities of rum. The effect of the alcohol gradually becomes evident. He engages the other drinkers in conversation, becoming in turn talkative, then argumentative and finally aggressively overbearing. His theme becomes personal and he bemoans his stupidity in marrying young, losing his freedom and having to support a wife and child. Prompted by the outside voice of an auctioneer selling off the remaining horses of the day, he comments that he can't see why men can't get rid of wives they don't want by selling them 'as these gypsy fellows do their old horses'. We gather from his wife's remonstrances that he's 'talked this nonsense in public places before'.

A swallow has entered the tent and flies to and fro over people's heads. Befuddled eyes follow it idly. The conversation has been disjointed and now lapses altogether. Time passes and the company degenerates.

The husband returns to his subject, offering to sell his wife to the highest bidder. His wife implores him to stop his nonsense and another period of silence ensues. Once more the husband rouses the drinkers, asking for someone to act as an auctioneer and for his wife to stand up and show herself. One of the women present tries to intervene but a volunteer auctioneer is found to play along with the stranger's drunken caprice. He promptly receives an offer of 5/-, which gets a laugh. The auctioneer suggests a guinea but receives no response and the husband says he'll not sell for less than five. The auctioneer repeats the offer: 'Do anybody give it? The last time. Yes or no?'

'Yes', says a loud voice from the doorway.

A sailor steps forward, places five crisp Bank of England notes on the table and clinks down five one-shilling coins on top of them.

Stunned silence. With the demand and response of real cash the drunken frivolity of the scene disappears. "A lurid colour seemed to fill the tent, and change the aspect therein. The mirth wrinkles left the listeners' faces, and they waited with parted lips."

Hardy has prepared us very carefully for this highly dramatic scene, gradually feeding us the information we need to understand his characters' situation and relationship. He takes his time over the build-up to the climax of the first chapter. Although based on an actual happening, Michael Henchard's sale of his wife, Susan, is a bizarre occurrence, but Hardy knows that his readers' acceptance of its credibility is crucial to the success of his story. *The Mayor of Casterbridge* is a human tragedy, the story of a successful man destroyed by a combination of ill-luck and his own mistakes and personal flaws. None of the examples of this popular literary theme that I've subsequently read have quite come up to the impact that this one made on me. Probably an instance of first love.

The teaching of my school exam texts was didactic and unimaginative and at one stage the class spent several lessons writing down verbatim a dictated chunk of a scholarly work on Hardy, probably someone's Ph.D. thesis. In this instance, however, I wasn't put off: I had the stirrings of an interest in literature, or at least in the works of one acclaimed novelist.

Soon after this epiphany I received a geography prize, the consequence of obtaining a distinction in the subject in my second attempt at school certificate (first time round, geography had been one of the subjects I'd failed). Distinctions were a bit thin on the ground in geography, a very low status subject not studied by boys designated by the school as academically able. In a rare touch of liberalism, prize-winners were allowed to choose the book with which they'd be presented on speech day. My geography master would, I imagine, have assumed I'd select a scholarly geographical text, perhaps an analysis of Mollweide's map projection which we'd spent an inordinate time studying, but he didn't comment on my choice – Thomas Hardy's *Tess of the D'Urbervilles*.

I suspect that the rural setting of Hardy's novels contributed substantially to their accessibility for me. Literature, of course, is one of the ways in which we learn about other people and about worlds of which we have little or no knowledge. However, it also provides us with another view on a world that is familiar to us and so deepens our understanding of the life we ourselves are leading. I was a country boy steeped in the ways of the countryside. I knew what a hay-trusser was and had seen turnip-hoers at work in the fields opposite where I lived. Moreover, in my later teens when I was reading *The Mayor of Casterbridge, Tess of the D'Urbervilles* and *Far from the Madding Crowd* I was a casual farm-worker, a clear case of poacher turned gamekeeper, or, at least, scrumper turned paid cherry-picker.

The rural England of Hardy's Wessex novels would be unrecognisable to a farm worker today, but that wasn't the situation in the 1940s. Many farming tasks at the time of the Second World War were carried out by hand, just as they were in the 19th century. During summer weekends and school holidays I learnt to handle a pitchfork and billhook, to pick up potatoes at speed before the plough came around again, and to re-stack sheaves of corn into their little pyramids after they'd been beaten down in the fields by wind and rain the night before. I can still visualise the barn in which I spent what seemed like weeks shovelling a mountain of corn from one end to the other to allow the air to get to it.

On rare visits to Buckinghamshire over the years, I've occasionally passed the farm which provided most of my work nearly three-quarters of a century ago, sparing a glance for the successor to the hedge that I painstakingly pruned, carefully half-cutting through the major stems and folding them over to provide a neat woven top of still-live branches. The last time I drove that way, the current hedge had been 'pruned' in the modern style, with a mobile cutting machine that had indiscriminately hacked and shredded the branches. It looked like the mutilated remains of a stretch of battlefield vegetation.

Thomas Hardy was a quintessential Englishman. Born in a hamlet near Dorchester, where his father was a stonemason and local builder, he lived in Dorset for most of his life, featuring the county in his Wessex novels. He was much influenced, both as a novelist and poet, by George Eliot and the Romantic poets, especially William Wordsworth. Hardy was a champion of the countryside and the people who lived in it. His characters' lives are bound up in the land and often restricted by factors beyond their control – the weather, the conditions under which they work, the class system and the declining status of rural people.

Hardy's heroes and heroines are usually the victims of their own passions, but, when they are in trouble, they find themselves in a hostile world in which they are forced to recognise, with Susan Henchard, that anything is possible 'except perhaps fair play'. Keenly aware of the social constraints on the lives of those living in England in Victorian times, Hardy was outspoken in his criticism of the traditional views of religion, education, sex and marriage that caused ordinary people much unhappiness and suffering. His reforming zeal aroused considerable middle-class antipathy. *Tess of the d'Urbervilles,* for example, was condemned for its sympathetic portrayal of a 'fallen woman' and was initially refused publication. *Jude the Obscure* received an even more negative response and some booksellers sold it in brown paper bags. One bishop allegedly burnt a copy of the book, causing Hardy to observe that the prelate was presumably in 'despair at not being able to burn me'.

I was deeply moved by both *Tess of the D'Urbervilles* and *Jude the Obscure*, but it was *Two on a Tower*, a much less well-known novel, that actually reduced me to tears, the only time that I can recall succumbing to such unseemly behaviour as a young man. I can recall the occasion quite clearly. I was on a post-national-service refresher course and had reached such a crucial stage in the narrative that I felt justified in reverting to my sixth-form days and cutting a parade I should have attended. I hid away in an Aldershot barracks changing room and snuffled my way through several chapters.

Two on a Tower is a romance, a story of a love relationship that breaks virtually every nineteenth century taboo. Lady Viviette Constantine is a mature, married woman who falls in love with Swithin St Cleeve, an attractive young man eight years her junior. She is a conventional and religious member of the aristocracy. Her lover is working class, idealistic, single and agnostic. Viviette is fully aware of the consequences of flouting Victorian social conventions, but cannot resist temptation and, after the death of her husband, the couple decide to marry. She persuades Swithin that they should conceal their marriage until he has achieved a degree of social status through his scientific work. This is never going to work and leads to a succession of problems and disappointments. As so often in a Hardy novel, sheer bad luck contributes to the misfortunes of the main characters so that it appears as if Fate and Chance are conspiring against them.

There is an added dimension to *Two on a Tower*. Swithin is an astronomer and, in his own words, Hardy sets ' the emotional history of two infinitesimal lives against the stupendous background of the stellar universe'. In so doing, the author inevitably invites comparisons between the vast openness and promise that the lovers view through the telescope and the constraints and confinement they are experiencing here on earth. Viviette and Swithin are 'star-crossed lovers' in more ways than one. Hardy's novels often convey a sense of the relative insignificance of human lives within the greater scheme of things.

2.

Fate and Fortune

Thomas Hardy must be credited with first awakening in me the realisation that the reading of English Literature is an enjoyable and rewarding experience. He was, however, ably supported in this process by his contemporary, Joseph Conrad. I became attracted to Conrad's works whilst on a 15-month sojourn in the Malay archipelago, the setting for his first two books, *Almeyer's Folly* and *The Outcast of the Islands*.

One of the compensations of the compulsory national service required of young men after the Second World War was that it offered conscripts the possibility of foreign travel at the Government's expense. I was naturally keen to exploit this opportunity as fully as possible. The Army actually interviewed national servicemen to ascertain their preferred destinations after basic training, but I had learnt the hard way that such consultative processes had little substance. When called up for national service, I'd been asked if I had any preference of regiment and, in accordance with the tendency of grammar school boys to have an inflated opinion of themselves, I'd expressed an interest in the Intelligence Corps, with the Education Corps as second choice. Presumably noting my height (just under 6'3" at the time), the interviewing officer assigned me to the Military Police, second only to the Pioneer Corps in the league table of least attractive options. Based on this experience, when next asked to state a preference, I put in a strong request for a home assignment, the opposite of what I wanted.

I was pleased with my posting to Singapore and Malaya, as it was then called, and intrigued by my exotic equatorial location and the lotus-eating lethargy that it induced in the Malay people. Conrad's writing was strongly influenced by his maritime travels, and wonderfully rich in its descriptions of the tropical countries that he visited towards the end of the nineteenth century. It was the setting to his novels that prompted me to read *Almeyer's Folly* and *An Outcast of the Islands* and the impression they made on me led to my then reading *Heart of Darkness, Lord Jim* and his later work, *The Rover.*

There are many iconic figures in history who have achieved distinction after a difficult and unpromising childhood but Joseph Conrad (born Jozef Teodor Konrad Korzeniowski) must surely rank as one of the most remarkable. A Polish exile, he was 20 when he took up British citizenship and began to learn our language; he was in his late thirties by the time he produced his first novel. Yet he became one of the greatest masters of English prose of all time. Joseph's father was a political activist who suffered persecution by the Russian rulers of the part of Poland in which the Korzeniowski family lived. Joseph had no formal schooling and was tutored at home by his father. Orphaned at 11, he was taken in by an uncle who eventually obtained a place for him at a boys' boarding school, although he attended for less than a year. He was considered intelligent and well-read, but proved to be a difficult pupil who showed little inclination to study.

From an early age Joseph longed to go to sea, an ambition fulfilled at the age of 16 when he joined the crew of a French ship as an apprentice. He remained a mariner for 19 years and eventually became a captain, by which time he was serving aboard British ships. Throughout his life, Conrad suffered from ill-health – both physical and mental. He experienced frequent depression and at the age of 20 attempted suicide by shooting himself.

I was fortunate in coming to Conrad via his first two novels. He's not the most accessible writer to anyone who is just beginning to read literature, for his characters are enigmatic and mysterious and his meaning often ambiguous. Yet, ironically, most young people are introduced to his work via the novella, *Heart of Darkness*, his shortest but in some ways most elusive work. Dickens is similarly treated, with *A Christmas Carol* deemed a suitable school text on account of its brevity: it is of course a heartwarming story, but the tedious passages of moralising are enough to put teenagers off literature for life.

I was 20 when Conrad's genius impinged on me, but other writers were vying for attention by this time and some of Conrad's works remained inexplicably on my 'must read' list for many years. The catalyst for re-connecting with this remarkable writer was *The Secret Agent,* one of several purchases from the bookstall at a local village fête. It's a very pertinent read at the present time, the central character being engaged in helping to protect the social and political systems of western countries from subversive elements seeking to destabilise them.

Colin Toibin is just one of the writers and critics who have pointed out that Conrad's fiction, written 100 years ago, anticipated subsequent World events. Great authors hit on universal truths concerning the human situation, which inevitably means that their works speak to future generations, as well as their own. Encouraged by my enjoyment of *The Secret Agent,* I bought a copy of *Nostromo.* Over the years critics who like to grade an author's works have raised this highly imaginative story of Man's vulnerability and corruptibility to pole position in the list of Conrad's great works. I can understand why.

The main characters in *Nostromo* are obsessives, driven remorselessly by some over-riding commitment or desire. Thus they owe much to the characters in a Ben Jonson comedy or the flawed heroes in a Shakespearian tragedy. But, unlike their Elizabethan and Jacobean stage predecessors, Conrad's obsessives are complex characters, described and fully analysed in a way that enables us to appreciate what lies beneath the surface and how their predominant passion has taken hold of them. Crucially, too, they are capable of change and development, three-dimensional characters in whom we can believe and who are recognisable in our own world. The villains, in particular, have clear 21st Century counterparts.

Conrad presents a masculine view of a male world in his novels, which is not perhaps surprising in someone who spent nearly 20 years at sea. Women don't receive the same attention as men, but they are, nevertheless, characters to be reckoned with and Emily Gould in *Nostromo* is someone with whom it is easy to empathise. Moreover, there are moments of sensitivity and gentleness between men and women in this novel that show another side of the author. The breadth and range of Conrad's skills as a writer are clearly evident in *Nostromo*. The love scenes, the delightful descriptions, the occasional little satirical touches, all contribute to the feeling that he has moved up a gear in this novel.

Impressive as *Nostromo* is, if I had to recommend just one Conrad book it would be *Victory*. At the centre of this rarely-mentioned novel is the fascinating but elusive character, Alex Heyst, who has inherited his father's belief that the conventional ways in which Man strives for happiness only bring pain and disillusionment. Heyst's solution to this dilemma is to eschew normal human relationships and to avoid putting down roots or establishing friendships and romantic or sexual relationships. He exists on the fringe of society, observing the normal social and business interaction of others with a detached air of amusement. The novel's dramatic tension stems from two encounters that threaten Heyst's studied detachment from everyday life. Ironically, both of these are the consequence of acts of gratuitous generosity by Heyst himself that initiate precisely the kind of relationship that he is normally so careful to avoid. With his defences breached, Heyst finds that his inexperience handicaps him in dealing with these new situations.

Victory is full of surprises, not only in the twists and turns of the plot, but in its constant shifts of pace, focus and perspective. The lengthy philosophical passages in which Heyst and Lena struggle to analyse and express their love for each other are intellectually demanding – but well worth the effort. And the reward is that the narrative picks up excitingly again, or the exotic setting explodes on our senses with another vivid description, or there'll be an entertaining satire on Victorian values, or even a laugh-out-loud riotous situation. This novel seems to have it all.

Hardy and Conrad apart, my choice of reading material in the two-year period immediately after leaving school was arbitrary and idiosyncratic. I had only the vaguest knowledge of our country's literary heritage. I could name some famous writers and 'great works' but knew little about them and wouldn't have been able to assign authors to their centuries or genre, or to distinguish between their various works. What I did have was a clean sheet and the time to set about covering it.

The period of initial training that eighteen-year-olds encountered as national servicemen was full-on and utterly exhausting, but there was often a significant falling off in the pressure once the brutal initiation was over. While waiting for my posting after initial training, I had considerable time to myself during which I read *Oliver Twist*, John Masefield's autobiographical account of life *In the Mill*, Priestley's 'Time Plays' and, most appropriately, Rudyard Kipling's *Barrack Room Ballads*. Later, in Malaysia, I found that policing responsibilities alternated with quite generous periods of free time. Night duties, for example, were normally followed by a full twenty-four-hour rest day, which enabled me to explore the area in which I was stationed, and also to pursue my newly-found leisure time activity. I don't think I realised at the time just how fortunate I was to have this freedom and how instrumental it was in my developing the reading habit.

There was another feature of army life that I have come to realise was invaluable to me – the emphasis on the importance of teamwork. My secondary school cultivated an habitual competitiveness in its pupils. We were constantly driven to outdo each other in regular tests, and then praised or castigated according to our position in interminable ranking lists showing our academic status within the class. Some of today's secondary schools have taken this approach to such extremes that all their effort is put into grooming their pupils for national exams, the consequence of which is that many other important facets of education struggle for recognition, or are ignored altogether. A particularly sad example is the low priority given to developing children's love of books, reflected in the frequent inclusion of libraries in the cost-cutting exercises instigated by both schools and local councils. Many children enter the secondary stage of education as avid readers of fiction and yet leave after A-levels unaccustomed to opening a book not connected with their specialist studies.

National Service brought a relief from the obsession with competition by focusing on an entirely different set of priorities. In the army one learns the importance of working effectively as a team, co-operating rather than competing with other people, building trust and confidence in others, providing support for weaker members. I played a lot of sport as a teenager and this, coupled with my farming experience, meant that I was already reasonably fit when I entered the forces. The physical challenges we faced in initial training were therefore not quite so daunting for me as for some raw recruits. One of my strengths was as a long-distance runner and I remember I rather looked forward to seeing how I fared in our first six-miler in full battle dress and carrying a brick-filled backpack. However, I quickly learnt that these exercises weren't races, with adulation for winners and abuse for losers:

they were team exercises in which we worked towards a situation in which every member got home in the prescribed time. The better runners had a responsibility to support the weaker ones, to pace and encourage them and track backwards and forwards trying to keep the group together.

I recently listened to a radio programme in which two bright young MPs who had been army officers before entering politics were sharing thoughts on their transition. One was Conservative, the other Labour, but they had an identical view of the House of Commons as a place where people were constantly jockeying to draw attention to their own importance and potential: the 'look at me' syndrome, they termed it. They agreed that many of their colleagues wouldn't last long in the army, or indeed any other organisation where people have to work co-operatively to get results.

Somewhere between the beautiful show-piece city of Singapore and its vast no-go area of stinking alleyways which the Military Police patrolled at night, I found a dingy candle-lit second-hand bookshop. Here I browsed among the confusion of unrecorded and unclassified literature, not really knowing what to look for, but emerging after each visit with a pile of assorted reading material determined largely by what was available. Uninformed and indiscriminate, I purchased a wide assortment of books, once again not confining myself to novels but including short stories, poetry and plays – Shakespeare's tragedies and comedies, Ben Jonson, Sheridan, Oscar Wilde, George Bernard Shaw and Emlyn Williams. I returned to barracks with some strange collections. In one of these, Mrs Gaskell's compact little *Cranford* nestled between the copious *Posthumous Papers of the Pickwick Club* and a complete set of Guy de Maupassant's short stories (in translation). The total absence of anything modern was no doubt significant. RGS syllabuses were all historically-based with little or no reference to a subject's modern applications: I can't recall any of the scholars who taught us English ever acknowledging the existence of contemporary literature, let alone recommending that we might find some of it interesting and relevant. The second-hand Singapore book-shop appeared to be caught in the same time-warp, or perhaps I was simply conditioned to regard the modern fiction section as an irrelevance.

I had a number of good friends in the army, but no-one with whom I felt I could discuss the books that I was reading. My fellow soldiers, if they read at all, had not progressed beyond the comic and newspaper stage and, as a late-developer myself, it wasn't for me to think less well of them for that. However, I was unsure of how they would react to my own blossoming book-reading interest and so, not wanting to appear an oddball, I pursued my hobby in secret. The barracks where I spent most of my time abroad shared a site with the Singapore International School and, although this establishment was of course locked when the school was closed, the classrooms were accessible simply by scaling the high outside walls and climbing through the unshuttered spaces between wall and ceiling that provided ventilation in a stifling equatorial climate. I spent many hours of uninterrupted solitude in this sanctuary.

I did find someone with whom I had a conversation of sorts about books. He was an Indian bearer employed as a general batman to carry out some of our more routine kit-cleaning chores. His British education under the Raj had given him an impressive facility in quoting extensively from the classics but not, unfortunately, much insight into the works that he'd studied. Things looked up, however, following a footballing accident that left me with a torn ligament which took a long time to heal. I was ten weeks in a military hospital and, during this time, met two people who were far more used to the pleasures of reading than I was. Occupying a bed next to mine was a badly-wounded private soldier, a Fijian shot fighting for the British in their struggle against insurgents on the Malayan mainland. He was one of the most impressive and interesting people that I've ever met and, although clearly in great pain, he talked lucidly and profoundly on a range of subjects. He preferred autobiography to fiction and was partway through Winston Churchill's Memoirs the week that he died. My other companion was the ward sister who, in addition to discussing books with me, provided me with a steady supply of classics – Jane Austen, Trollope, Thackeray, George Eliot, the Brontë sisters and Mark Twain.

I'm a comparatively slow reader and this was the first time that I'd been able to read a novel at a single sitting. It's a very different, more intense experience than the normal situation in which the reading of a book runs over several days, or even weeks. Some books make their greatest impact when read at one go. There are, of course, others that are simply far too long for that – Margaret Mitchell's *Gone with the Wind*, for example, or Tolstoy's epic historical novel of the Napoleonic campaigns, *War and Peace*. Many lengthy books were originally written for serialisation and so lend themselves to the reading of an episode at a time. Hardy's *Two on a Tower* is an obvious example and most of Dickens' novels came out in monthly instalments.

Some books clearly require a lengthy period of time not only to read but assimilate. Once started, Vikram Seth's mammoth family saga, *A Suitable Boy,* takes over one's life. Despite its length (1474 pages) this novel moves at a cracking pace. The central theme is introduced immediately:

> " 'You too will marry a boy I choose,' said Mrs Rupa Mehra firmly to her younger daughter. Lara avoided the maternal imperative by looking around the great lamp-lit garden of Prem Nivas. The wedding-guests were gathered on the lawn. 'Hmm,' she said. This annoyed her mother further. 'I know what your hmms mean, young lady, and I can tell you I will not stand for hmms in this matter.' "

The Mehras are an upper caste Hindu family. Mother is a widow who, having successfully arranged her eldest daughter's marriage in accordance with Indian custom, turns her attention to finding a suitable boy for her younger daughter. Lata, however, presents her mother with a much bigger challenge than that of her docile sister who had been happy to go along with the tradition of arranged marriages. She's a student at Brampur University, a quiet girl, but unpredictable and with a mind of her own.

The tension between Hindu custom and modern westernised views of marriage runs through the novel: we meet Lara's various boyfriends and student companions, her mother's choice of a suitable boy and three other large families with links to the Mehras. The book has a myriad of clearly-delineated characters from the ruling class – landowners, businessmen, politicians, managers, members of the judiciary and the university world, and of course their families. There are numerous loosely connected narratives and a variety of themes concerning the exercising of authority, power, status and influence – within the family, in business and professional life, in politics and religion, in rural communities and urban society. *A Suitable Boy* provides a colourful and panoramic view of India in the second half of the 20th century shortly after Independence and Partition. Vikram Seth introduces us to many facets of his country – its conflicts, enigmas and paradoxes, its traditions, religions, politics and power bases, the marked differences between rural and urban communities, features of business and professional life, and the country's music, clothing and food. The book is an educational experience, fiction on a grand scale. It's a book to savour and reflect upon over a period of time and it will live in my memory for years to come.

As a student I was, I'm ashamed to admit, a thoughtless mutilator of books, annotating texts to such an extent that the contents were sometimes submerged by my additions. I have learnt to be much more respectful and protective of my books and rarely add a pencil mark to anything that I'm reading. I do, however, use half a sheet of blank paper as a bookmark and occasionally make notes on points of particular interest. Soon after starting *A Suitable Boy* I decided that I'd never be able to remember all the characters' unfamiliar names and so began listing them, together with a reference to their role. I confined myself to those characters who looked destined to play a continuing part in the narrative. There were 56 of them.

Fifty years after national service, I again had the leisure time to read successive books at one sitting. As before, the enforced leisure resulted from an accident, this time the trouble being what is commonly called 'a slipped disc'. My wife, Jill, and I were visiting our eldest daughter, Sarah, in New

England on the occasion of the birth of our second grandson. 'One-sitting' was actually a misnomer on this occasion as the only way in which I could get relief from pain was to lie flat on my back, which I did for hours on end, sometimes with three-week old Patrick sleeping peacefully on my chest. It was obviously not a position from which to read anything very heavy, in terms of either weight or subject matter.

The very civilised town of Ridgefield in Connecticut, where we were staying, boasted an excellent book-shop with well-read staff with whom you could discuss books and receive informed advice on new authors who might be of interest. Via members of my family I stocked up with the works of several up-and-coming American writers who hadn't at the time impinged on the British market, although some have done so since.

Elizabeth Strout had just published her first novel, *Amy and Isabelle* – a lively and quite erotic story of a mother and her teenage daughter. It's full of incident and insight into human relationships and there are some splendidly entertaining minor characters. Sue Miller's *The Good Mother* and Jane Hamilton's *A Map of the World* provided frightening reminders of how unforeseen tragedies can completely change our lives and affect our relationships for ever. Both concern the loss of a child and involve a pivotal court case, the outcome of which owes more to the skill of the lawyers and prejudices of those who sit in judgement than the rights and wrongs of the situation under scrutiny.

Alice McDermott was another new name to me. Her novels also have a strong sense of the arbitrariness of life, starkly illustrated in *After This* by the way in which a quarter of American young men were drafted into the army to fight in the Vietnam war, some never to return and others so seriously affected by their experiences that they were unable to resume normal life. Alice McDermott presents her characters and their relationships through the observations and recollections of relatives and friends, including children. She has a sure touch with her characterisation and dialogue.

I very rarely abandon writers after having read just one of their books and I continued reading further works by all the authors whom I sampled during my days in bed in New Hampshire. Sue Miller has been particularly rewarding and the Bloomsbury Publishing Company deserve credit for bringing her books to the notice of the British public. She's a writer who admirably demonstrates the good novelist's ability to bring us closer to fictional characters than we can get to real life friends and acquaintances. Her novels present us with the myriad incidents, thoughts and memories that make up people's lives – the moments of joy and sadness, the crucial turning points and decisions they've taken, the mistakes made and the opportunities missed. She deals with universal and everlasting aspects of the human situation: the shifting perceptions that we and others have of the past, the struggle to reconcile our past and present selves, the need to expiate our sins and errors of judgement and to seek forgiveness; the conflict between the search for truth and justice and the expediency of compromise and acceptance of things as they are. Sue Miller's novels open our eyes to the nuances of human emotions, widen our sense of sympathy and compassion, and deepen our understanding of our own existence and relationships.

Although there are numerous recurrent themes in Miller's novels, the stories are distinctive and the characters drawn from different backgrounds and age groups. For example, *When I Was Gone* concerns a past tragedy – a murder – that took place in a commune of liberated young people and returns to haunt one of its members in middle-age, threatening to destroy her marriage. *The Lake Shore Limited* features a play of that name and opens with its first performance; the play resonates with all the characters, who are either cast members or present in the first-night audience. *The Distinguished Guest* is a story of an old lady who has a book published at the age of 72 and becomes a public figure as a result of its success. *The Senator's Wife,* to which I've returned more than once, analyses a subtle network of relationships revolving round the marriage of a successful politician and his wife. The title of *Lost in the Forest* refers to the search for happiness and a coherent meaning in life among a group of characters who sense that their lives are running out of control. It's a very good introduction to Sue Miller's fiction for those who don't know this American writer. There are some superb passages dealing with a teenager's state of mind and emotional turmoil after the sudden death of the step-father she loves.

This is an author who has an instinctive feel for the key events and big moments in a novel – sparing in her use of set pieces, she knows when and how to use them to maximum effect, without dwelling on them for too long. This restraint is a great strength: she doesn't over-dramatise or manipulate situations for gratuitous effect or simply to further the plot. There's a refreshing absence of literary devices and tricks of the trade. In short, she has absolute integrity. I particularly like the way she builds up the tension and expectation of a big moment and then eases off so that the drama that we think we've seen coming fizzles out – as it often does in real life. This self-discipline and refusal to take the easy option heighten the impact of the dramatic scenes when they are fully developed. Sue Miller's novels present us with that delightful dilemma of conflicting desires that all readers of fiction experience on occasions: the urge to read on apace to see what happens next, and the counter wish – to linger over each chapter to prolong our intimacy with characters whose lives we want to go on sharing.

Another American writer with a keen insight into everyday human relationships is Pulitzer prize-winner, Anne Tyler. Her much-loved stories of Baltimore family life focus on a basic human dilemma – the need to connect and bond with other people and the conflicting desire for freedom and independence. Her families are invariably quirky and dysfunctional, but fundamentally decent and likeable people with whom we readily empathise. Interviewed at the age of 75 about possible subjects for her next novel, Tyler was asked whether she'd be making any mention of Donald Trump. "I think of writing," she replied, "as a visit to a thoughtful, reasonable world where people try to be kind to one another. I can't imagine how I could ever fit Trump into that."

We're not experiencing English Literature on a grand scale in Tyler's novels. They're not concerned with political intrigue or corruption, or set against a backcloth of national or international events. There are no huge dramas or Titanic struggles between the forces of Good and Evil, or between Man and the Elements. We're not challenged by ratiocination, symbolism or hidden layers of meaning. There are no great mysteries, extra-sensory experiences or visions of the future, no foreign quotations or classical, Biblical and historical references. And, although Anne Tyler writes extremely well, she's not a stylistic or structural innovator. Nowhere do you get the feeling of a writer 'deforming his medium in order to say what has never been said before', which, according to Sophie Denoël in Coetzee's *Summertime,* is the mark of good writing.

Anne Tyler's achievement is to make the ordinary extraordinary, to create a fictitious middle-class world in which we recognise many of the human situations that influence our own lives. She has a long-established cult following and, after the publication of each new book, authors and reviewers queue up to praise her. John Updike pronounced her 'not merely good but wickedly good'; Nick Hornby, Roddy Doyle and John Boyne have all nominated her 'the greatest living novelist writing in English.' I doubt if anyone's reading is sufficiently all-embracing to enable them to make a judgement like that, but it's always worth noting what authors say about other writers. There can't be many novelists who can match her achievement in consistently delighting readers with her penetrating and compassionate portrayal of ordinary family life. I don't often have a dud experience in my reading but, if I feel that a book I've just finished has been truly disappointing and unrewarding, I find re-reading one of my favourite Tylers an excellent therapy.

Academia tends to be snooty over authors whose subject-matter is small-scale, particularly if their literary skills are unobtrusive and unpretentious. The prestigious *Oxford Companion to English Literature* provides a perfunctory 40-word paragraph on Anne Tyler's achievement, compared to a 1,500 entry for the 18th century novelist, Lawrence Sterne. There's a detailed analysis of Sterne's main work, *Tristram Shandy*, 'a slim story constantly interrupted by digressions on a huge variety of scientific and philosophical matters.' It's not exactly an irresistible recommendation but no doubt the digressions provide endless material for post-graduate research.

3.

Small Lives and Teeming Worlds

"It is a truth universally acknowledged that a single man in possession of a good fortune must be in want of a wife."

The playful irony of the opening to Jane Austen's *Pride and Prejudice* has made it one of the most-quoted sentences in English literature. It epitomises the whole novel, which has a youthful exuberance and unrestrained comic insight that have delighted millions of readers. It is certainly my favourite Austen, although I rate Emma as Jane Austen's most likeable heroine and I understand the critics' regard for *Persuasion* as her most mature and well-written work. My special affection for *Pride and Prejudice* stems in part from its being the first book to open my eyes to the way in which a skilful writer handles dialogue to reveal characters and their relationships. The novel is a master class in this respect.

Despite her narrow field, Jane Austen has always occupied a high position in the canon of English literature. Her modern successors have not been so fortunate. British writers such as Barbara Pym, Elizabeth Taylor and Anita Brookner have all tended to be undervalued and stigmatised for being 'limited', not limited in their perception and portrayal of the nuances of human behaviour and interaction, but narrow and unadventurous in their choice of subject. They are seen as dedicated chroniclers of small lives.

All three of these authors people their books with characters, women in particular, who lead placid and genteel lives largely undisturbed by the turbulent world outside their immediate circle of relations, friends and acquaintances. As Mildred, the narrator in Barbara Pym's *Excellent Women,* observes,

> "I wondered that she should waste so much energy fighting over a little matter like wearing hats in chapel, but then I told myself that, after all, life was like that for most of us – the small unpleasantnesses rather than the great tragedies; the little useless longings rather than the great renunciations and dramatic love affairs of history and fiction."

Barbara Pym was, by all accounts, a modest and unassuming person, not unlike some of her heroines. When writing one of her novels she said she hoped it would provide an interest for her friends. In fact, she achieved a much wider readership than that: after initial rejections of her first book, she found a respected publisher in Jonathan Cape and the early books were well-received. There was then a puzzling 14-year hiatus when Cape declined to accept any more of her works and she was unable to find another publisher. The reason given was changing tastes: both the content and the style of her books were deemed old-fashioned. Yet that hadn't worried a lot of people.

I was aware of Pym's novels before I read them, as my mother empathised with both the author's worlds – that of the books and the not dissimilar one that Barbara Pym herself inhabited, as revealed in her autobiography. A single parent, my mother had a hard life and Pym gave her a glimpse of a lifestyle far removed from her own and yet one that, had things worked out differently for her, she might conceivably have experienced herself. The lives of Pym's characters may be uneventful, but their genteel and comfortable routine was something to which my mother always aspired. Had the small-town businessman who took her out for rides in his horse and trap not been married, my mother might conceivably have become his wife, rather than being left to bring up his child on her own.

Pym continued writing throughout the fourteen-year period during which she was unable to find a publisher, stockpiling the novels of her latter years. Support for her work in the academic and literary world remained strong. John Bayley, writer, critic and Oxford professor of literature, described himself as a 'dreamy devotee, moving daily in a Pym world' and fondly reading bits of the novels to his wife, Iris Murdoch. Iris was apparently 'patient and unappreciative'. However, Bayley had other allies in the literary world who were instrumental in bringing about a dramatic change of fortune for Barbara Pym, albeit just three years before her death. The turning point came with a powerful article in *The Times Educational Supplement* championing her work and written jointly by historian Lord David Cecil and poet Philip Larkin. Publishing re-started and a stream of novels came on to the market, some of them posthumously. The author's reputation grew apace, both here and in America.

Barbara Pym writes consistently well. *Excellent Women, A Glass of Blessings, Quartet in Autumn, The Sweet Dove Died, A Few Green Leaves* – all receive special mention by one critic or another. I'd add to these *An Academic Question* and *Less than Angels,* both of which satirise university life. I worked for 14 years in Higher Education in four different universities, trying to change a culture obsessed with its self-importance and remote from the real world. Some of the conclusions that I came to during that time were very similar to Barbara Pym's; her views, for example, on the art of thesis writing:

> "A thesis <u>must</u> be long. The object, you see, is to bore and stupefy the examiners to such an extent that they will <u>have</u> to accept it – only if a thesis is short enough to read all through, word for word, is there any danger of failure."
>
> *(Less than Angels)*

The academic community gets some rough treatment from Pym, which somewhat belies her image as a 'gentle' satirist:

> "There are no sick people in North Oxford . They are either dead or alive. It's sometimes difficult to tell the difference, that's all."   *(Crompton Hodnet)*

Elizabeth Taylor didn't encounter the problems that Barbara Pym experienced with publishers, but still acquired the dubious reputation of being 'best known for not being better known'. When I first came across her work I thought momentarily that Elizabeth Taylor, the actress, had made a dramatic change of career, rather as she had consistently done with husbands.

The author apparently lived under the shadow of <u>the</u> Elizabeth Taylor and received a good deal of her namesake's fan mail, including requests from male admirers for photos of her in a bikini. On one such occasion her husband suggested she should send one and give 'her' fans a surprise, to which she replied, 'I don't have a bikini.' Another unobservant male, presumably.

Elizabeth, the author, was mildly amused by the glamorous life she lived vicariously through her misdirected fan mail, but she had no desire for the public attention given to her namesake. Although married, she was a very private person, even closer to her fictional characters than Barbara Pym was to hers. She too had strong support from other writers and critics, among them Ivy Compton-Burnett, Elizabeth Jane Howard, Angus Wilson and the critic, Robert Liddell. Ann Tyler is among her more recent admirers, who also include Paul Bailey, Sir Kingsley Amis and Sarah Waters.

Knowing nothing of Taylor's novels at the time, I chose randomly for my first experience of her work. One of the last of her twelve books, *Mrs Palfrey at the Claremont,* is set in the Claremont Hotel on the Cromwell Road, where a small community of elderly and mildly eccentric gentlefolk see out their last days. They lead extremely quiet and trivial lives, trying to fill the tedious hours between meals with knitting, reading, crossword puzzles. It's the 1960s and TV is conspicuous by its absence.

As Jonathan Cape said of Barbara Pym's *An Unsuitable Attachment,* it's a picture of a world we tend to associate with the past. Yet that world hasn't actually gone away. Much as we may wish to, we can't dispense with old age. In fact, it's more prevalent, and its problems, frustrations and sadnesses occupy an ever-increasing part of our lives. Elizabeth Taylor captures the reality of this situation with great sensitivity and humour, tempering her astute satire with understanding and compassion. Her characters are not always lovable, but we are skilfully guided to an understanding of the reasons for their caustic comments and unkindnesses as they fight their corner, seeking to keep up appearances and retain some degree of control of their lives.

Mrs Palfrey at the Claremont opens with the main character's arrival at the hotel:

> "She was a tall woman with big bones and a noble face, dark eyebrows and a neatly folded jowl. She would have made a distinguished-looking man and, sometimes, wearing evening dress, looked like some famous general in drag."

Any new arrival at the Claremont creates a stir and Laura Palfrey makes an immediate impact. Taylor uses such events to animate her characters and reveal their foibles and prejudices. The satirical skill that she shows in managing group interaction revolving round key characters is reminiscent of Jane Austen, and presumably one of the reasons she is sometimes likened to her more illustrious predecessor.

Anita Brookner, the third of my small group of expert 'chroniclers of small life', seems to me the most remarkable of the three. Her origins have resemblances to Joseph Conrad's. Born in 1928 in Herne Hill, she was the only child in a Polish immigrant family. Her parents changed the family name from the Germanic-sounding 'Bruckner' to 'Brookner' because of anti-German sentiment in Britain. They were secular Jews who offered a home to fellow immigrants seeking refuge from German persecution during the 1930s and WW2.

Anita had a lonely childhood with early caring responsibilities for her parents – 'transplanted and fragile people' whom she felt she had to protect. She did well at school and university and pursued a very successful academic career as an art historian. She was the first woman to hold the post of Slade Professor of Fine Art at Cambridge University and was subsequently appointed Reader at the Courtauld Institute, where she taught and researched until she retired in 1988. She was awarded the CBE in 1990.

An established writer of art histories, Anita Brookner produced her first work of fiction in 1981 – when she was 53. I became an early admirer and waited impatiently for each new novel to appear in paperback. Fortunately, the waiting was never protracted: in a twenty-year period Brookner produced at the rate of almost a novel a year. She slowed slightly in her late seventies, but was still writing in the years immediately before her death in 2016, when she was 87.

The early novels established the agenda for which Brookner became famous – the uneventful lives of single women who long for a more outgoing personality and a more interesting and rewarding lifestyle. Her heroines see around them lively, self-assured and attractive people whom they would like to emulate and whose company they wish they could share. Above all, they regret the absence of romance in their lives: they want to be loved, to be the centre of someone's attention, and to find true companionship. When precious opportunities for the realisation of these dreams arise, they tend to be half chances, easily misunderstood and mishandled. Too much significance is often paid to any sign of male attention, no matter how tentative. In two of the early novels, *Providence* and *Look at Me*, the heroines' hopes are dashed in a particularly painful and unexpected way. The novels are psychological studies of how her characters come to terms with the harsh realities of their lives, the disappointments and the rejections. Although sad characters, Brookner's heroines are usually resilient and stoical, able to develop defensive strategies that enable them to retain some self-esteem.

This easily-recognised stereotype of a Brookner novel actually does the author a disservice, for each book has subtle variations of situation and character that make it distinctive. She is constantly introducing new insights and characters to sharpen our awareness of her world. In *Visitors* the catalysts are a group of young men and women, a singularly unattractive trio who nevertheless cause Theo May, the book's central character, to re-examine her routine and priorities. *Family and Friends* is a story of a mother and her four children, two of whom are conformist and caring and two wayward and self-indulgent. The heroine of *Closed Eye* is married to a respectable man old enough to be her father, her only experience of passion coming when she meets the attractive husband of a friend. More significant than these variations in Brookner's heroines is that a quarter of her novels – the equivalent to the total output of some writers – have a male central character.

Anita Brookner's most widely read novel is *Hotel du Lac*, but that is simply an anomaly of the book award system. Early novels by new and very promising writers often find their way onto the shortlist of annual competitions such as the Booker Prize, and sometimes get the judges' nod ahead of the works of established authors. *Hotel du Lac* was a surprise winner of the 1984 Booker, ousting the strong favourite, J G Ballard's *Empire of the Sun*. Anything that encourages new writers is, of course, to be welcomed and it's good that the various prizes for outstanding novels are spread around. One slightly odd consequence of this policy, however, is that the judges only rarely make a second award to a winning author, so that young writers who become prize-winners at the beginning of their career acquire a reputation based on an early novel, rather than on their later and, often, more mature works. The bodies responsible for these awards will, of course, point out that they are simply choosing the outstanding novel in a particular year, not passing judgement on the status or overall achievement of authors. However, the reading public sees it differently: it's invariably the prize-winning novels that are the most widely read and discussed and which have the strongest influence on the author's reputation.

The game of 'name the author's best work' is a somewhat pointless exercise and virtually impossible with prolific writers who maintain a consistently high standard. Ann Tyler's *Breathing Lessons* won the Pulitzer Prize in 1989. It wasn't an early work, but an example of what she was producing in the middle of her career. She has continued writing for another 30 years and her most recent novel, *Clock Dance*, came out in 2018. My guess is that those who have had the pleasure of reading all her books wouldn't come to the conclusion that *Breathing Lessons,* good as it is, was her most outstanding achievement. Her own favourite is *Dinner at the Homesick Restaurant.* The same point could be made with regard to Ian McEwan's *Amsterdam,* which won the Booker Prize in 1998. Several of his subsequent books have reached the six-title short-list in recent years and I have no doubt that one of them would have been a winner had *Amsterdam* not got in first. There has certainly been no falling off in the standard of his writing in the past 20 years.

Anita Brookner has constantly refined and improved her skills as a writer of fiction and most of her later novels are models of English usage. *Undue Influence*, written in 1999, is just one example of beautifully modulated and seamless prose. The language is precise and clear, devoid of ornamentation or ambiguity. Brookner's craftmanship is significant, but entirely unobtrusive, as if it were the most natural thing in the world. The first paragraph of *Undue Influence* admirably demonstrates her art :

"It is my conviction that everyone is profoundly eccentric. Those people I pass on my way to work every morning almost certainly harbour unimaginable fantasies. Nor are my neighbours entirely to be trusted. Once my mother and I were disturbed by the sounds of a ferocious altercation coming from the flat above ours in Montagu Mansion, yet the following day we were able to address our usual greeting to the stately widow who lived there and who was visited, as far as we knew, only by her son, an economist at the Department of Trade and Industry. Shortly afterwards she informed my mother that she was going to live with her son in Maida Vale. This was somehow understood to be a sensible arrangement, arrived at in a mature manner, although to judge from that epochal argument it seemed less than reasonable. She was in the habit of looking in on my mother, who rarely left the flat. 'Poor boy, his marriage did not work out,' she said, with a lovely show of tolerance, but my mother reported the gleam of victory in her fine eyes. She had promised to keep in touch after she moved, but my mother died and the widow failed to put in an appearance. I dismissed this as normal behaviour, and was able to do so because by that time I had come to realise that most people are entirely inconsistent and that one is advised to treat them gently, keeping one's scepticism to oneself. Not to let it show is a desideratum of civilised behaviour.''

From the very first Austenesque sentence – seemingly matter-of-fact but teasingly paradoxical – we are alerted to the linguistic delights to come. The illustrations that follow qualify the opening statement, explaining and softening the paradox. The narrator and her reflections on human nature are economically developed and by the end of the paragraph we are comfortably ensconced in the familiar Brookner world.

The number of female novelists who focus on the day-to-day relationships of ordinary people suggest some special female interest and insight into the emotional side of people's lives. This is somewhat dangerous debating ground likely to arouse entrenched views on the differences between the sexes. However, it is clear that the qualities that characterise the work of Barbara Pym, Elizabeth Taylor and Anita Brookner are not unique to female writers. There can, for example, be few authors of either sex who can improve on William Trevor's understanding of the complexities, paradoxes and mysteries of the human situation: the bitter-sweet mix of happiness and suffering; our vulnerability to chance circumstances and timings; the legacies of the past and uncertainties of the future; the regrets of past opportunities and dreams of what might have been; our essential solitariness and insignificance in the greater scheme of things.

The Story of Lucy Gault, one of William Trevor's last novels, will always live in my memory. It's a painfully sad and, at times, melancholy tale with characters so full of warmth and goodness that we are moved to love as well as pity. It's finely crafted and quietly narrated, yet full of surprises, tension and suspense. Set in the first half of the twentieth century, it presents an evocative picture of a bygone age and a lovely rural setting cut off from the outside world by the absence of all the channels of communication we have today – a situation very important to the plot. The prose is elegant and perfectly in tune with the novel's time and mood.

William Trevor wrote some 40 novels and collections of short stories over a fifty-year period. They feature a broad sweep of characters from different classes, environments and age groups, including working-class Irish girls and public school alumni, small farmers and representatives of the Dublin and London professional class, life's successes and failures, the elderly and the vulnerable, and the corrupt who prey on them.

Colm Toibin, another Irishman and a contemporary of William Trevor, presents an even wider range of characters. *Norah Webster* is one of his most recent novels. It's a gentle, restrained story of an ordinary woman who loses her husband. We follow her grieving and her efforts to protect her family from the inevitable difficulties arising from her widowhood. Norah is determined to maintain her independence in the face of the well-meaning, but often unwelcome, attempts of relations and friends to advise and take control of her life. These may appear slender resources on which to arouse and maintain a reader's interest, but Toibin is wonderfully sensitive to character, mood and the hidden nuances of human relationships. He is also another writer who makes the difficult art of communication appear almost effortless.

The Master, one of Toibin's earlier works, is a fictional portrayal of the American author, Henry James. In one sense it's very much Anita Brookner territory, with a central character whom we meet as an adult and accompany through a middle-age in which opportunities for a deep and lasting human relationship are missed or fail to develop. However, *The Master* is a more complex, lengthy and subtle exploration of the single state than its typical Brookner equivalent. Also, of course, Henry James was a highly successful author, admired and fêted by the wealthy and famous, and in Toibin's novel he clearly has more control over his life than Anita Brookner's heroes and heroines have over theirs. Indeed other people want more from Henry than he wants from them. Nevertheless, he comes to regret his failure to respond to some of the overtures others have made towards him. Brookner's heroes and heroines don't usually receive the overtures.

Norah Webster's and Henry James' characters and lifestyles are entirely different. *The Testament of Mary* presents an even greater contrast. It's a highly dramatic re-imagining of the most powerful tale of all time – the crucifixion and the events surrounding it, told through the eyes of Jesus's mother looking back on it years later. Toibin's Mary is a strong heroic figure determined to tell the truth about her son's brutal death and to resist the attempts of Jesus's followers to glamorise and embellish it for their own ends. When at the climax to her story she scornfully rejects the virgin birth and the whole concept of her son's being the son of God the blasphemy is shockingly powerful.

Two of Toibin's novels, *The Master* and *The Story of the Night,* raise the problem of dealing with the homosexual identity. Toibin, however, doesn't allow his own situation as a gay, male writer to define the focus of his work as a whole. *Brooklyn,* for example, is a delightful love story of a young Irish girl's sexual awakening and journey into adulthood. If you didn't know otherwise, you'd have put money on its having been written from personal experience. My sixteen-year-old grand-daughter is currently reading the novel: she was astonished when I mentioned that the author was a man.

William Trevor's and Colm Toibin' s novels introduce us to a range of characters and sections of society. Some authors try to do this not by the variations between their different works but within a single big novel. John Lanchester's *Capital* is one example. It's set in Pepys' Road, a fictional street in Clapham which is presented as a microcosm of 21st century London. Lanchester is clearly intrigued by the great mix of nationalities and cultures found in our cosmopolitan capital city. The characters resident in Pepys' Road , or in some way connected with it, include a highly-paid investment banker and his wife, an elderly widow who has lived in the street for most of her life, a Pakistani family who live above their convenience store, a highly-educated asylum-seeker from Zimbabwe who works illegally as a traffic warden, a young Singalese footballer who lives with his father and plays for a Premier League club, and a builder from Warsaw working on some of the properties.

Anyone attempting to convey London's diversity is likely to suffer by comparison with Dickens' crowded pictures of its Victorian counterpart. A typical Dickens' novel ranges across the upper, middle and lower classes of society and all the many variations in between that defy classification. The location is frequently London. *Our Mutual Friend*, one of his later and, I believe, under-rated works, is a good example. There are representatives of various professions – including of course that Dickens' bête noire, the law – and a whole host of menial and middle class occupations. There are schoolteachers and clerical assistants, a lawyer and barrister, a pawn shop assistant and the mistress of an inn, a money-lender and various financial wheelers and dealers, a taxidermist, a ballad seller, a dustman, a child-minder, a doll's dressmaker, a lock-keeper and a waterman who scours the Thames for bodies that may have a few coins in their pockets. The idle rich are also well represented. Not only are they all brought vividly to life as characters, but the ways in which their lives are defined by their work, environment and income are very evident.

In any consideration of a novelist's breadth and variety, Charles Dickens is likely to be placed at one end of the spectrum, and Jane Austen and her modern counterparts at the other. The one features a kaleidoscope of very different characters and 'worlds'; the others concentrate on a precise and limited field. Colin Toibin and William Trevor come somewhere in between: they range much more widely than the 'chroniclers of small lives', but are both quieter and less busy novelists than Dickens.

All these very different writers do, however, share one very important feature: they are extremely interested in people and their accurate representation in fiction. Colin Toibin could well be speaking for them all when he says that his primary interest as a writer is in his characters. The extent to which these writers make us believe in their characters is more important than the breadth of their canvas.

4.

The Novelist as Satirist
and Political Activist

It's a cloudless summer's day today: the deckchair beckons and I'm tempted to occupy it for an hour or so with Carson McCullers' *Ballad of the Sad Café*. It's a skilful story full of unexpected developments, apparent paradoxes and revelations. McCullers keeps the reader guessing, gradually releasing information on her characters and past events, but always holding something back so that we are never sure of the significance of each new situation or to what it will lead.

On reflection, I decide to remain indoors and head for the usual upright chair in my study: I want to lose myself in the story and not be distracted by midges, the neighbour's grinding lawnmower, the application of suncream etc. Philip Roth, author of *American Pastoral*, a sombre and disturbing novel on the disintegration of the American dream, declared that 'reading literature requires silence, some form of isolation and sustained concentration.' That's perhaps overdoing it a bit, but he has a point.

I ask my wife if I'm a reclusive reader and she replies: ''You used to sit inside the playpen to read the newspaper when the children were at the crawling stage.'' Ah well, perhaps my hours with Dickens and the Brontës at a formal classroom desk in Singapore conditioned me to solitary reading.

I'm a slow reader and like to absorb the detail of a book. A facility to skim-read is useful when seeking information, but it's not appropriate for fiction. There are inevitably times when writers wander off-course a little, but in a well-written novel very little is gratuitous. The events and characters interact like pieces of a jigsaw, gradually forming a coherent whole as the book progresses. Descriptions of a story's setting – the country and its history, the district, the precise scene of the action – all have a role to play in establishing our understanding of the characters and their story.

In some novels, of course, the setting plays a major part in the plot, influencing events and characters' reactions to them. For example, in *Waterland*, Graham Swift's atmospheric and gripping novel about the Fens, the landscape and its history are a very powerful force in people's lives. In rural novels the weather is often a significant factor, none more so than in Hardy's Wessex novels where it can assume the role of a malevolent character thwarting people's hopes and aspirations. In Jon McGregor's *Reservoir 13* the passage of time, as marked by the changing seasons, is key to our understanding of the action. *Prodigal Summer* by Barbara Kingsolver tells a series of stories about a group of farmers and conservationists whose relationship with the land that they tend and protect is as important as the human dramas that unfold.

The character of particular buildings, streets, landmarks can be very significant. Places that were used as the setting for famous novels of the past are invariably preserved and attract many visitors. Local politicians and tourist agencies are quick to see the business potential when a best-selling novel is set in their area, especially if it's followed by a film version of the book. The list of best things to see in Saint-Malo, Brittany, now includes the places in the town that were so important to Marie-Laure, the blind girl in Anthony Doerr's stunning 2015 Pulitzer-Prize Winner, *All the Light We Cannot See.*

Readers of novels need to be alert to all sorts of small details that may not appear particularly important when they're introduced, but which are later seen to be significant. Even Dickens with his episodic way of writing was well aware of the need to prepare his readers for subsequent events. A good book merits the reader's undivided attention.

Authors obviously make extensive use of their own experiences in their novels but, once bitten with the writing bug, they frequently look at other people's worlds for ideas. The result is a seemingly endless range of options for readers. Name a subject – alchemy, motor-cycle maintenance, perfume, garden mazes, tattoos, the London sewage system – and you'll find it featured in someone's novel. When writers explore new ground, their research skills are obviously put to the test. The challenge for novelists introducing a specialist world is to acquire just sufficient knowledge to establish their characters' credibility. They must guard against becoming too immersed in the specialist jargon and detail, lest they end up like many academics – unable to communicate with those who have little background knowledge of their specialism.

Ian McEwan is one of the most adventurous of outstanding modern novelists. All his books are different, most of them spectacularly so. He combines a sharp intellect with meticulous research and writes with impressive authority on different specialist fields. *The Children's Act* takes us inside the consciousness of a successful High Court Judge. In *Saturday* the central character is an eminent neurologist; *Solar* features a renowned physicist. *Enduring Love* is a suspense-filled thriller in which the main character is pursued relentlessly by a man suffering from erotomania or Clérambault's syndrome, a delusional condition that causes people to believe that someone has fallen deeply in love with them. Nearing the end of his career, McEwan is becoming increasingly unpredictable and innovatory – his 2016 *Nutshell* is a re-telling of Shakespeare's *Hamlet* from the point of view of an unborn child.

You never feel that you've got the measure of McEwan: each successive novel extends the range not only of his subject matter, but of the skills he shows in writing about it. Even when he has chosen a seemingly familiar topic, his handling of it is always distinctive and original. *On Chesil Beach* is a dramatic and very moving account of a young couple in the 1960s who, although very much in love, find themselves unable to consummate their marriage. The story focuses on Edward and Florence's disastrous wedding night with flashbacks to their courtship and a desperately sad final section on 'what might have been' that brings to mind William Trevor's *The Story of Lucy Gault*. McEwan is surefooted and confident throughout, an author at the height of his powers. Characters and events are sharply defined, almost photographic in their impact. The structure of the novel is cleverly conceived, the intense and painful drama of the wedding night suspended from time to time as we learn more of the characters and their relationship during courtship. It's a serious novel but there are some memorable tragi-comic moments. There is a great deal going on beneath the surface – clues to the direction in which the plot may (or may not) develop, hints of possible violence, incidents from the characters' childhood that might have had a bearing on their relationship. The book leaves the reader with a strong sense of human solitariness and the struggle we all have to communicate our thoughts and feelings accurately.

On Chesil Beach is set in the year 1962, before the significant easing of the pressure that young people used to be under to conform to clear boundaries and social conventions in their sexual relationships. In 2017 the film version of the book was released and in a subsequent interview McEwan, who was the screen writer for his own novel, answered questions on the extent to which the problems faced by young lovers in 1962 were relevant to today's romances. He felt that, whilst the sexual revolution had, to some extent, liberated British youth and provided a language with which to talk about sex, it had not succeeded in making young people's relationships much easier:

> "Today's young people are under terrifying pressures, completely different from the kind of pressures that Edward and Florence face in 1962....We need to pause and consider what the relationship is between sexual experience and emotional bonding....That's such a powerful thing and I think young men are being fed a purely pornographic notion of what it is to love someone....Young boys in their teens are seeing unbelievable, athletic pornographic stuff on the internet which really warps their expectations....There are

huge pressures on young girls to be a certain shape, wear certain things, be in a certain style of whatever and deliver, without much discussion of the emotional truthfulness or affection or kinds of emotional play that would provide the real peak of sexual experience."

McEwan went on to comment on a study that had recently shown that one in eight young people do not have sex until their late twenties. "The most commonly given reason," he said, "is the fear, the pressure of expectation. People are just a bit worried that they'll fail, they just won't measure up to the expectations."

Another novelist interested in the sexual revolution is the American author, John Irving. *The 158-Pound Marriage* tells the story of two couples who are drawn into wife-swapping and inevitably get badly hurt in the process. Irving is an American author just as difficult to classify as Ian McEwan. His novels are imaginative, original, well-researched and cover a wide range of inventive settings and situations. His plots twist and turn with suspense, menace and the unexpected; an underlying threat of violence occasionally becomes a reality. As in a McEwan novel, the sex scenes are explicit. His characters tend to be subordinate to the plot, but they're sharply drawn and always interesting. Irving writes 'big' books, in every sense of the word – two or three times longer than most of McEwan's works and full of action. The mood shifts constantly, ranging from thought-provoking insights into human behaviour to comic scenes reminiscent of *Monty Python*.

The Fourth Hand is a good example of both Irving's fertile imagination and his skill in changing the mood of a novel. It tells the story of a promiscuous New York TV journalist,

Patrick Wallingford, who has his left hand eaten by a lion during the filming of an interview at a zoo. The Lion Guy or Disaster Man, as he becomes known, has a transplant which leads him into a peculiar, but ultimately fulfilling, relationship with the widow of the donor of his new hand. As a condition of the transplant, Doris Clausen, the widow, had demanded access rights to the donated hand to enable her to relive her relationship with her ex-husband, particularly his manual dexterity in their love-making.

The first half of the book is full of comic characters and situations and Patrick Wallingford's sexual adventures figure prominently. His partners are athletic and innovative in bed, but their activities are frequently interrupted by abusive phone calls from other women and, on one occasion, from members of the partner's family. Among several memorable characters, there's the surgeon who replaces Patrick's hand, a Doctor Zanac, whose skill in removing dog turds from the towpath with his lacrosse stick is not appreciated by passing rowers.

As Patrick's relationship with Doris Clausen develops, the tone and nature of the novel change. Patrick falls in love and undergoes a process of soul-searching and redemption from which he emerges a better person. In short, he makes the transition from a purely physical appreciation of sex to what, in his 2017 interview, McEwan referred to as 'emotional bonding'. The love story is told with tenderness and sensitivity.

There's a further dimension to this entertaining novel. The book is a sharp satire on the media – its role as self-appointed arbiter of public morality, its constant focus on the trivial and sensational, and its unacceptable intrusion into people's lives. I read *The Fourth Hand* at a time when several British newspapers were under close scrutiny over their frenzied and libellous character assassination of one of the men questioned by the police investigating the murder of the Bristol landscape gardener, Joanna Yeates. As a result of this real-life situation, Irving's view of the media resonated particularly strongly with me.

Irving has a keen satirical eye for the ambivalence of human behaviour. A major theme in *The Cider House Rules* concerns the rules by which we ostensibly live and work, and the principles – or lack of them – that actually determine our behaviour. The title of the book refers to a list of rules posted in the cider house of a company called Ocean View Orchards. The black migrant workers who pick the apples are expected to adhere to these published instructions. However, they can't read, and their working routine is actually governed by the rules made, and constantly broken, not by the company but the migrants' enigmatic overseer, Mr Rose. This juxtaposition of theory and reality recurs throughout the novel. There is the law and then the ways in which we justify breaking it; the code of conduct that we establish for ourselves in our daily routines and relationships, and the reasons why we deviate from it. Some of the characters establish their own procedures for workers to follow and will countenance no deviation from their personal demands.

The Cider House Rules is vintage Irving, a no-holds-barred tour de force dealing ostensibly with abortion, but ranging widely in its action, characters and themes. Irving's acknowledged admiration for Dickens is particularly evident and accentuated by quotations from and references to *David Copperfield* and *Great Expectations*.

Authors who push the boundaries inevitably risk disappointing or alienating some readers and both McEwan and Irving are no strangers to controversy. Nothing, of course, divides a readership more clearly than an explicitly political novel. Robert Tressell's *The Ragged-Trousered Philanthropists* is a classic of working class literature which has acquired cult status with the politically left-wing. Those of the opposite persuasion are unlikely even to have registered its existence.

Robert Tressell was a painter and decorator called Noonan, the pen name being a reference to the trestle table which was a basic part of every interior decorator's equipment. Noonan contracted tuberculosis and had to give up his painting and decorating. He then spent his time writing a novel based on his own experiences as a member of the working class, always battling with poverty and the threat of the workhouse. *The Ragged-Trousered Philanthropists* is a passionate attack on the subjugation of the working class and a heartfelt plea for a new political system. Frank Owen, the central character and author's mouthpiece, conducts a personal crusade to explain to his workmates precisely how they are exploited by the upper- and middle-class and how socialism could bring about a more equitable distribution of the wealth that their work creates.

Owen finds the task he has set himself a challenging one, for he is expounding concepts that his fellow workers find very difficult to understand. An even greater problem is that the men are deeply imbued with the idea that it is the natural order of things for the rich and powerful to govern and manage, and for the poor to accept orders and to labour. They constantly grumble at their treatment and the inadequacy of their wages, but nevertheless accept that this is their lot and they can do nothing about it. Owen's hatred of the system and those who habitually exploit it for their own ends is matched by his intense exasperation at the ' not for the likes of us' attitude of his fellow workers. His conclusion is that the reluctance of the men to try to understand or better their situation amounts to a passive form of philanthropy. He is vitriolic in his condemnation of churches, schools and charitable organisations for what he sees as their systematic indoctrination of ordinary people into accepting their inferiority.

The Ragged-Trousered Philanthropists provides a picture of social, economic and political life in the early 20th century when socialism was beginning to gain ground. The human stories that the novel tells are free of sentimentality and exaggeration, the characters distinctive and three-dimensional. Given the strength of his passion, Tressell shows surprising discipline in avoiding any over-dramatising of events: he lets situations speak for themselves, but is skilful in heightening their impact by sowing seeds and rousing the reader's expectations. By using his central character and some of Owen's political associates to expound their socialist doctrine, Tressell makes the book's message an intrinsic part of the narrative, rather than a series of intrusions by the author.

Tressell finished his novel in 1910 but was unable to find anyone prepared to publish it. Disillusioned, he decided to emigrate to Canada, hoping that his daughter, with whom he lived, would be able to join him later. However, having set out for Liverpool, he became seriously ill before he was able to board a ship and died of his tuberculosis. He was buried in a pauper's grave. Three years after his death, Tressell's daughter found a publisher for his book, although to do so she had to agree to extensive cutting that involved the removal of most of the socialist doctrine. It wasn't until 1955 that the unabridged version of the book became available to the public.

The American equivalent to *The Ragged-Trousered Philanthropists* is John Steinbeck's *Grapes of Wrath,* which describes the plight of migrant workers from Oklahoma driven off the land in the Great Depression of the 1930s. Steinbeck describes one family's journey to California where there is the prospect of work in the State's prolific orchards and cotton fields. Here they are caught up in a system designed to bring maximum profit to the large landowners, canning factory owners and banks. Thousands of families clamour and compete for work in order to survive, and employers exploit this situation by forcing workers to labour for a pittance. Any sign of protest or discontent is brutally crushed and those who attempt to organise unions are taken into custody.

The obscene contrast between the abundant crops and poverty of the people is angrily exposed by Steinbeck:

> "The people come with nets to fish for potatoes in the river, and the guards hold them back; they come in rattling cars to get the dumped oranges, but the kerosene is sprayed. And they stand still and watch the potatoes float by, listen to the screaming pigs being killed in a ditch and covered with quicklime, watch the mountains of oranges slop down to a putrefying ooze; and in the eyes of the people there is the failure; and in the eyes of the hungry there is a growing wrath. In the souls of the people the grapes of wrath are filling and growing heavy, growing heavy for the vintage."

The Grapes of Wrath became a best-seller, but was strongly criticised for its political stance. Steinbeck was attacked as a propagandist and socialist and the Associated Farmers of California denounced the book as a 'pack of lies'. Steinbeck, however, had visited the workers' camps when writing his novel and vehemently maintained that his book accurately portrayed their inhumane treatment and the way in which their spirit had been crushed.

The political novel that is currently going round in my head is *The Ministry of Utmost Happiness* by the political activist and author of *The God of Small Things*, Arundhati Roy. In the celebrated opening to *A Passage to India* E M Forster presents two contrasting pictures of a fictitious Indian city. One is the illusion of lush parkland that visitors and tourists receive from the hillside overlooking the burgeoning toddy palms, neem trees, mangoes and peepul. The other is the reality when you descend the hill, stand below the city's canopy and see the mean dwellings seemingly of 'mud moving, so abased and monotonous one feels the Ganges should wash the excrescence back into the soil.' Arundhati Roy pays passing tribute to India's beauty in *The Ministry of Extreme Happiness* but her focus is on the dreadful reality of life in this vast country dominated by class and caste, where millions live in abject poverty, routinely subjugated and brutalised because of the accident of their birth. Roy gives a deeply disturbing insight into a country where many people's aspirations are simply to survive, in defiance of their daily persecution and appalling living conditions.

Arundhati Roy takes the lid off this toxic situation in a way that neither E M Forster nor Vikram Seth attempted. *A Passage to India* looks at the country through the eyes of white colonialists and their contacts; *A Suitable Boy* is a saga featuring members of the Indian ruling class and upper caste. Roy writes on behalf of those at the bottom of the hierarchies of society, class and caste and it's an uncomfortable read.

Readers who don't warm to her political message will feel that her rant against oppression, corruption and bestiality goes too far, dwelling on the extremes of inhumanity – in the way that political activists campaigning for a fairer and more just world are inclined to do. Critics will have probably been joined by some ardent admirers of *The God of Small Things* who had waited two decades for Arundhati Roy's second novel and may well have felt that the political themes of *The Ministry of Utmost Happiness* were prioritised at the expense of the fascinating love story involving the enigmatic Tilo and her three admirers, Musa, Naga and Biplab Dasgupta.

There is a danger of Arundhati Roy's distressing picture of a society at war with itself having the same effect on a western readership as the daily TV news bulletins cataloguing the latest instances of human misery in far off lands. Warm and comfortable in our modern homes, we watch, appalled yet detached – for what can we possibly do to help stem the processes that create these tragedies? But Arundhati Roy's condemnation of India's divided society has implications for us all. Corruption, injustice and abuse of power are features of all societies, including our own western democracy. Their prevalence and intensity, however, vary enormously from country to country. We are extremely fortunate to live in a society where we all have a voice. It's not always listened to, but it's still influential. In many countries all dissent is ruthlessly crushed and any writer expressing an alternative political view faces imprisonment or assassination. We need to guard our precious democratic right to protest, otherwise we could lose it.

There's a tendency in our country for the silent majority to rely on small groups of activists to fight society's battles for justice and fairness. This considerably weakens the process of protest: Liverpudlian families had to campaign for 27 years before it was admitted that responsibility for the Hillsborough football stadium disaster lay firmly and squarely with the police and the design of the stadium, not with the football supporters, as had been persistently alleged. It remains to be seen whether we learn from that example and give the Justice for Grenfell Protest Group proper support to ensure a speedier outcome of their efforts to establish the truth over the Grenfell fire in 2017. Every victory for those who exercise our right to campaign for a fairer and more just society is important, no matter how trivial. Well done the Bournemouth residents who provided 'extensive feed back' to their council, suggesting that there are more humane ways of dealing with the homeless than fitting bars on park benches to prevent their being used for sleeping purposes.

Any consideration of the political novel as a genre is bound to include reference to the enormous contribution that Charles Dickens made to our understanding of the very big differences in the quality of life experienced in Victorian times according to the strata of society to which people belonged. Dickens' huge output of lengthy novels provides a panoramic view of the divisions in our society and a vivid picture of the squalid conditions in which so many people lived in the nineteenth century. 'Dickensian' has subsequently become a word used to describe an unacceptable level of poverty.

Dickens wasn't as insistent a political campaigner as Robert Tresswell and Arundhati Roy in calling governments and society to account for the failings of the system. He wrote about many facets of society that inevitably included scenes of poverty and degradation, and situations in which the rich and powerful exploit the weak and vulnerable. His compassion is obvious, but the political message is not quite so direct and continual as that of the habitual campaigner. Perhaps Dickens' method is the more effective.

Dickens' novels teem with characters, ranging from the saintly to the utterly despicable. The fact that some of his most memorable creations are eccentrics and grotesques shouldn't blind us to the fact that he had a remarkable insight into human nature and behaviour. This, of course, helps to explain the continued popularity of his novels today, nearly 200 years after they were written. He writes, as he always maintained, about real life, and speaks not only for the age in which he lived but also for that which we now inhabit. Thus the schools in *Nicholas Nickleby*, in which unwanted children were abandoned to cruelty and neglect, are forerunners of those 21st century orphanages and children's homes that have been found guilty of abusing the young people in their care.

Dickens featured a wide range of institutions in his novels – children's homes, schools, factories, workhouses, prisons. One of the most memorable is Thomas Gradgrind's school in Coketown in *Hard Times*. Dickens didn't have to invent this establishment: it is a straight copy of actual schools run at that time by two societies for educating the poor. These schools were totally utilitarian and run along factory lines; in fact they were often overseen, as in Coketown, by a mill owner. The method of learning was derived from the Catechism: children were drilled with military precision in groups of facts in the form of dictionary-type definitions. Dickens simply took this real life model and applied his wonderful comic imagination to expose its absurdity and pernicious consequences.

The novel opens with a classroom scene. Gradgrind is visiting and showing off to a government inspector. He is re-iterating the methods required of the school to the schoolmaster, Mr M'Choakumchild, who has no doubt heard them many times before:

> "Now what I want is, Facts. Teach these boys and girls nothing but Facts. Facts alone are wanted in life. Plant nothing else, and root out everything else. You can only form the minds of reasoning animals upon facts: nothing else will ever be of service to them."

Gradgrind surveys the little rows of pitchers waiting to be filled with facts and his eyes light on a new girl who is thrown into confusion by being asked to define a horse. Declaring 'girl number 20 unable to define a horse', Gradgrind then tries one of the boys, by the name of Bitzer, who comes up with the correct answer:

> " 'Quadruped. Graminivorous. Forty teeth, namely twenty-four grinders, four eye-teeth and twelve incisive. Sheds coat in the spring; in marshy countries sheds hoofs, too. Hoofs hard, but requiring to be shod with iron. Age known by marks in the mouth.' Thus (and much more) Bitzer."

Girl number 20 is told that she now knows what a horse is. But girl number 20, alias Cissy Jupe, probably knows more about horses than anyone else in the room, including the three adults, Mr Gradgrind, Mr M'Choakumchild and the Government Inspector. It has emerged, in Gradgrind's questioning of her, that Cissy comes from a 'horse-riding' show that is in town: horses are a constant part of her life, but when she starts to reveal her background she is quickly told that they don't want 'to know anything about that here'.

In a typical Dickensian touch, Bitzer and Cissy are both caught in a ray of sunlight that lights up part of the classroom. This sunbeam has the effect of irradiating the girl who, dark-haired and dark-eyed, seemed to receive a deeper and more lustrous colour from the sun shining on her; whereas Bitzer "was so light-eyed and light-haired that the self-same rays appeared to draw out of him what little colour he ever possessed."

If Dickens were alive today he'd find much of our current education system familiar territory for his satire. Over the last three decades successive governments have assumed increasing control of education from the centre, systematically reducing the influence of local councils and the teaching profession. As a consequence, educational priorities have given way to a political agenda strongly influenced by the desire of central government to emulate those countries that consistently occupy the upper reaches of the annual international league tables of exam results. Unfortunately, the countries concerned are mostly totalitarian states employing factory methods to achieve a utilitarian product remarkably like Dickens' Bitzer.

5.

Reality and Fantasy

The driving force behind people's reading varies greatly. Firstly, literature is a relaxation, a respite from the daily routine, similar to interests like gardening, tennis or amateur dramatics. But for many readers it's more than that, providing a chance to extend their real-life experiences through their imagination. We meet a wider range of people in books than those we know in real life and, significantly, become aware of what they are thinking and feeling. Novelists take us into the hearts and minds of their heroes and heroines, so that our relationship with fictional characters often seems more intimate than it is with our actual friends and acquaintances. Novels are a particular pleasure to those who live solitary lives: you're never entirely alone when you have a good book.

Many of us see reading as an essential part of our education, increasing our knowledge of the world and its peoples, and deepening our understanding of human behaviour and relationships. Novelists, of course write about imaginary people and situations, but they use their fiction to open our eyes to basic truths about the human situation. Then there is the diametrically opposite aim of those who read in order to escape the reality of human existence by being transported into a wholly make-believe world. It doesn't, of course, have to be an either/or situation: our reading may fulfil more than one of these purposes and also reflect changing circumstances, moods and the passage of time.

I like to think that I am catholic in my literary tastes: I frequently re-read the classics, but am quite happy to try new writers with no established reputation. I do, however, have one obvious gap or black hole in my reading habits, and it's one that I have been lazy over trying to rectify: I don't like fairy stories. Perhaps I sustained some psychological damage in my Miss Falkner days from her wretched Digger Gnome and his flipping pippity pebble, but, for whatever reason, the activities of little folk, hobgoblins, monsters and batmen have never much interested me as an adult.

I contemplate the complex mythical world of J R R Tolkien's *Lord of the Rings,* firmly ensconced in poll position in most lists of the 100 Best Novels of All Time. I register that, on both the 25th and 40th anniversaries of the Booker Prize, Salman Rushdie's *Midnight's Children* was awarded a special 'Booker of Bookers' prize for being considered the best of all Booker prize-winners. I note the phenomenal sales figures for J K Rowling's Harry Potter books. I stand in Foyle's, now Waterstone's, gazing in bewilderment at the shelves of Rowling imitators and lookalikes. And, quite frankly, I'm puzzled.

There are numerous categories or genres of book that I don't go out of my way to read – science fiction, ghost stories, detective fiction, for example – but I don't bypass them altogether and I can clearly see why readers get hooked on them. But I have to admit defeat on understanding the huge appeal of mythology and fantasy, even when it's as excellently written as it is by Tolkien and Rushdie. I have read *The Hobbit,* but have never been able to face the best-selling *Lord of the Rings,* which has established its own culture with a vast network of film versions, societies, publications, mailing lists and websites, all devoted to exploring the mythical Middle Earth and its inhabitants. I did get through *Midnight's Children* at the second attempt, but this was mainly to avoid appearing a wimp to my teenage grandson, who'd clearly enjoyed it.

The first half of this Rushdie novel is a gripping family saga told against the background of political events in India in the years following independence and partition. The legacy of the past, steeped in ancient superstitions, myths, legends and a plethora of religious beliefs, vies with the harsh reality of a newly-born secular state unable to cope with all the problems of abject poverty, short life expectancy, widespread corruption and brutal abuse of power. The book has a strong narrative and is full of dramatic set pieces, unique characters and vivid descriptions.

The 'midnight children' of the title are 1001 babies born in the first hour of August 15th 1947, the moment of India's emergence as a sovereign state. 581 of the original 1001 children in Rushdie's novel survive their first eleven years and at this stage of their development we learn that every one of them has a miraculous magical power of some kind. One is so beautiful that beholders are blinded if they look at her. There is a boy who has the gift of levitation and another with the ability to step into mirrors and re-emerge through any reflective surface. A Genoese girl is able, like Jesus, to multiply a catch of fish; there's a boy who can increase his size at will and a girl who can alter her sex whenever she likes. Many of the children are physically deformed and some are monsters. When these characters began to take over the narrative I gave up on the Booker of Bookers the first time round. It was at a similar half-way point that Rushdie apparently decided he'd had enough of George Eliot's *Middlemarch,* a book that absorbed me utterly the first time I read it.

I think it was an entry in *The Week* that made me realise just how far my view of pleasurable reading is from that of Salman Rushdie. Subscribers to this magazine will be well-acquainted with its 'recommended book' section in which well-known authors list half a dozen novels that they particularly admire. Salman Rushdie was asked to contribute and his recommendations were:

"*The Master and Margarita*: The devil comes to Moscow, accompanied by a cat shooting six-guns and an associate who disappears when he turns sideways.

The Sirens of Titan: A man, along with his dog, accidentally enters a chrono-synclastic infundibulum and gets stretched out across space and time.

Riddley Walker: The explosion of the '1 big 1' and the world after a nuclear explosion, written in brilliantly fractured prose as if the bomb has exploded there as well.

The Bloody Chamber: Sensual and erotic re-telling of well-known fairy tales, a blending of Snow White, Red Riding Hood and Beauty (of Beauty and the Beast).

Pedro Paramo: A man embarks on a journey and falls into a nightmarish world that may be populated entirely by ghosts.

The Non-Existent Knight: a suit of armour believes itself to be a knight."

It would be odd if writers of fiction, who spend so much of their time exercising their imagination, didn't fantasise ; thus it is not at all unusual for novels to include a mythological, supernatural or surreal dimension. I have no problem with that. In Alice Sebold's much-acclaimed first novel, *The Lovely Bones,* a murdered girl looks down from heaven and observes the effect of her death on her family. *The Fishermen* by Chigozie Obioma is a tragedy in which Macbeth's witches are replaced by a frightening madman whose terrible forecasts inexorably unfold. The narrator in Markus Zusac's *The Book Thief* is Death, God's servant charged with gathering up the souls of people departing this life. Macabre humour is often a feature of a surreal novel and Zusak's Death is a quirky and, at times, jokey character who is critical of the work-rate expected of him.

A popular form of fantasy with writers of fiction is to endow a character with a particular gift or inclination beyond that of a normal human being. Thus in Patrick Suskind's *Perfume,* a disturbing tale of depravity in eighteenth century Paris, the central character has a uniquely-developed sense of smell that enables him to detect and separate odours over incredible distances. In John Irving's *A Prayer for Owen Meany,* Owen, the main character, is a very strange boy, old and wise before his time. During a baseball match his best friend's mother is killed by a ball struck by Owen, who becomes convinced that this occurrence was no accident but that he had been an instrument of God. As this idea grows, Owen has what proves to be an accurate premonition of the time and manner of his own death and his whole life becomes a preparation for this event. In *Virgin Suicides,* Jeffrey Eugenides tells of five sisters who appear to be quite normal, but who have an enigmatic and elegiac quality that makes them mysterious and tantalisingly inaccessible to their admirers. The tragedy that ensues seems to be foreordained.

None of these novels has much in common with *Midnight's Children* with its huge cast of comic-strip characters capable of various magic tricks. Authors like to push at the boundaries of what is and isn't believable, but the deviation from the normally accepted realities of human behaviour in the novels cited are not so great that they undermine the books' credibility. Mind-reading, clairvoyance, premonitions of tragedy and death, the possibility of a previous and future existence, suicide pacts, people with one particularly highly developed sense: none of these is totally beyond the realms of possibility.

One of my brothers-in-law had severe learning difficulties and couldn't read the time or understand money. Philip was very withdrawn and, although he would respond hesitantly when spoken to, he never initiated conversation. His memory, however, was exceptional; for example, as an old man he could recall the name and address of a landlady he and his family had stayed with when he was a little boy. Whenever a member of the family was struggling to recall a past name, place or event they turned to Philip for help. Lupe, one of the characters in John Irwin's *Avenue of Mysteries* communicates only through her brother: no-one else can understand her. But she too has a particular gift: she is often able to sense what people are thinking and even sometimes relates situations that they have experienced in the past.

Readers, as well as authors, have powers of imagination. They are quite prepared to accompany authors into the unknown, particularly if the rest of the novel is firmly grounded in reality. It is commonplace to speculate on what past friends and relatives would think of current events were they still alive: it is not therefore a big leap to Alice Sebold's heaven-based narrator in *The Lovely Bones*. And in vivid accounts of the terrible carnage of war the introduction of a gruesome personified Death in *The Book Thief* isn't difficult to accept. One of the skills of an imaginative writer is to create a world where the normal and miraculous can co-exist.

However, Salman Rushdie's mixture of fantasy and reality doesn't work for me: it's too extreme. Rushdie admits that he has an uncontrollable desire to see just how far he can go in pushing the boundaries of credibility. Inevitably, there are casualties among his readers. Rushdie accepts this, in fact rather enjoys the situation. He appears to be as pleased with the reviews that, he claims, give him minus one out of ten as with those that give him eleven. There aren't apparently many in between.

Rushdie's usual explanation of his strange characters in *Midnight's Children* is that they symbolise the fantastic changes that have recently taken place in Man's perception of the World. His children are hallucinatory magical images that capture, metaphorically, the sweep and chaos of modern India and its resemblance to a dream or nightmare. Well…. maybe. I think I'm perhaps over-suspicious of intellectuals who seem to spend a lot of time pontificating on their own brilliance. I went off T S Eliot, another acclaimed genius who revelled in the obscurity of his work, when I read in my *Cocktail Party* programme one evening in the theatre that he didn't expect people to understand one of his plays until they'd read it twice and seen it three times. I am also suspicious of artists who flick oil paint onto their canvas from six feet away and then ride across it on a bicycle.

Fantasy is not the only way of representing the chaos of the world in which we live. If a teacher gives a class of teenagers an opportunity to write an essay on a subject of their own choosing, there'll normally be at least one or two dream sequences handed in. The work that defines this particular framework for me is Kazuo Ishiguro's *The Unconsoled,* a masterly merging of real and surreal worlds. Ryder, the main character, experiences a sequence of dreams in which he moves from one demanding situation to another, with frequent interventions causing sudden changes of plan and direction. He's habitually late for assignments, lost in a labyrinth of strange districts and streets – for example, cul-de-sacs with high walls at the end. Ryder is keenly conscious of his extremely busy schedule, but worryingly hazy about the detail. He is always being sidetracked away from his responsibilities and commitments by people vying for his attention.

I don't know what research Ishiguro undertook for this book, but the closeness of Ryder's nightmares to my own is uncanny and I imagine many of Ishiguro's readers must feel the same. The contexts are different, for Ryder is a concert pianist, whereas I had a teaching career; but the nature of some of the problems our minds grapple with at night are almost identical. My dreams are odd, but never funny: they're too full of angst for that. However, when similar situations are piling up for Ryder they make me laugh out loud. I suppose it's the banana skin effect.

A common feature of dreams is the way in which characters from one's past suddenly pop up, out of context and in unfamiliar roles. The instance that I especially enjoy in *The Unconsoled* takes place on a day on which Ryder is particularly haggled over finding time to rehearse for an evening concert performance that he is due to give in an unfamiliar European country. An additional worry concerns the arrangements for his elderly mother and father who are coming to hear him play. He has, however, had to set both anxieties aside as, in a borrowed car, he tries to find the way to the apartment that his wife is staying in to tell her that her father is dying and wants her to come to him immediately.

Ryder has left the town where the concert is being held and is speeding along deserted country roads. He realises he doesn't know the way to his wife's apartment and fears he's going in the wrong direction. Suddenly two figures emerge from woodland and signal him to stop. He pulls up and sees a group of people sitting on upturned orange crates drinking from tin camping-mugs. One of them comes across and joins the two by the roadside and Ryder recognises Geoffrey Saunders, an old schoolmate. Saunders is pleased to see him and asks if he'd join him and his companions in an important discussion they're having. Ryder's reply must rank as one of the great literary understatements of all time: "Quite frankly, Saunders, this isn't the best time for me."

Further delays occur as it transpires that there's been an accident to another pianist whom Ryder has met while abroad. Brodsky is about to have a leg amputated by one of Saunders' group, who happens to be a surgeon. They need Ryder's help and, after rummaging around in the boot of the car that he has borrowed, Ryder finds a hacksaw that the surgeon can use. The amputation is successful and Brodsky is able to walk with the aid of a folded ironing board which he uses as a crutch. There is never, of course, any hint that those involved in these surreal situations regard them as anything other than completely normal. There are some wonderfully entertaining moments in *The Unconsoled,* but it's essentially a serious work in which Ishiguro explores a wide range of human situations, predicaments and pretentions.

The reconciling of seemingly incompatible elements in a novel is a frequent challenge for authors. The combination of realism and fantasy is one example; the blending of the comic and serious is another. We read with mixed feelings of the amusing encounters that David Copperfield, Oliver Twist and other Dickens' innocents have with more streetwise characters who expose the boys' vulnerability. In the following scene, David recalls an occasion when Mr Murdstone introduced two of his acquaintances to him:

"We went to an hotel by the sea, where two gentlemen were smoking cigars in a room by themselves...

'And who's this shaver?' said one of the gentlemen, taking hold of me.

'That's Davy,' returned Mr Murdstone.

'Davy who?' said the gentleman. 'Jones?'

'Copperfield,' said Mr Murdstone.

'What! Bewitching Mrs Copperfield's incumbrance?' cried the gentleman. 'The pretty little widow?'

'Quinion,' said Mr Murdstone, 'take care, if you please. Somebody's sharp.'

'Who is?' said the gentleman, laughing.

I looked up quickly, being curious to know.

'Only Brooks of Sheffield,' said Mr Murdstone.

I was quite relieved to find it was only Brooks of Sheffield; for, at first, I really thought it was I.

There seemed to be something very comical in the reputation of Mr Brooks of Sheffield, for both the gentlemen laughed heartily when he was mentioned, and

Mr Murdstone was a good deal amused also. After some laughing, the gentleman whom he had called Quinion said:

'And what is the opinion of Brooks of Sheffield, in reference to the projected business?'

'Why I don't know that Brooks understands much about it at present,' replied Mr Murdstone; 'but he is not generally favourable, I believe.'

There was more laughter at this, and Mr Quinion said he would ring the bell for some sherry in which to drink to Brooks. This he did; and, when the wine came, he made me have a little, with a biscuit, and, before I drank it, stand up and say, 'Confusion to Brooks of Sheffield!' The toast was received with great applause and such hearty laughter that it made me laugh too, at which they laughed the more. In short we quite enjoyed ourselves."

Laughter begets laughter and we instinctively join in the general merriment, appreciating the quick wit and imaginative banter of Mr Murdstone's two companions. Yet the hilarity stems from a group of men making fun of a young boy and his blatant naivety and ignorance of the adult world. The joke is that David is completely unaware that 'the projected business' under discussion is Murdstone's wooing of David's mother ('the pretty little widow') and that the 'incumbrance' referred to is David himself. The treatment of David isn't malicious, but the men are having fun at a young person's expense and it's the sort of behaviour that in real life can easily become unkind. Dickens lets David tell his own story without adopting any moral stance as the author. But we learn later that Murdstone is a tyrant who shamefully abuses David, after pretending to befriend him as part of his tactics to win the affection of his mother. In retrospect, the scene is not as funny as it seems originally.

In re-reading this incident, I am again reminded of my brother-in-law, Philip, who was occasionally coaxed out of his habitual silence to tell us haltingly about his life in his care home. We gathered that he was sometimes teased by the proprietor of the home and we expressed some disquiet at this. Philip, however, assured us that he didn't mind, and his obvious enjoyment of being the centre of attention dissuaded us from taking any action. One day, however, when we were visiting, we were taken aside by one of the more mentally alert residents in his home who told us of her concern at a recent situation when Philip had been held up to ridicule. We took immediate action, feeling very guilty that we hadn't done so earlier.

There is a very thin line between comedy and tragedy, laughter and seriousness, and literature obviously reflects this in the way in which it often mixes the two. Some authors, of course, concentrate wholly on a comic view of life, maintaining a relentless satire on human failings and foibles, or relating the various adventures of a comic innocent who lurches from one absurd situation to another. P G Wodehouse invented a complete comic world with its own code of conduct and language. His novels, featuring the young gentleman Bertie Wooster and his indefatigable valet, Jeeves, acquired cult status and had a huge following. They were a forerunner of the popular TV series, *Yes, Minister,* much of the humour stemming from the juxtaposition of the languid stupidity of the man in charge and the superior knowledge and intelligence of the underling.

When reading comic novels, I find that my pleasure declines fairly rapidly if the comedy topples over into unremitting farce. The impact of a comic scene is greatest when it's rooted in reality and the funniest moments in fiction are often those that occur in serious novels. Howard Jacobson is a naturally funny writer and his *Coming from Behind* and *Peeping Tom* are, as their titles imply, both farcical romps. But a later work, *The Finkler Question*, is very different. A group of Jewish friends (and one Gentile) discuss Jewish identity, what it means to be a Jew – culturally, socially and ethically. They have very different views and their confrontational and dogmatic exchanges are extremely challenging – for each other and for the reader. However, despite its serious purpose, the book is consistently funny. It's significant that Harold Pinter, whose plays are such a fascinating blend of the hilarious and desperately serious was a big admirer of Jacobson.

The Truth about the Harry Quebert Affair, a lengthy and complex detective story written by the Swiss writer Joël Dicker, has much less claim to be a comic novel than *The Finkler Question*, but it features a prolonged episode that must rank as one of the most hilarious set pieces in contemporary literature. Marcus Goldman, the narrator of the story, is a bright and confident young American undergraduate with a burning desire to become a writer. He is convinced that to help further this aim he has to receive recognition of some kind – anything that will put the spotlight on him. His opportunity comes unexpectedly one day during a lecture given by Harry Quebert, a nationally-recognised author who is noted for his liveliness and originality as a speaker.

Quebert's subject on this occasion is one that is gripping America at the time – the Clinton-Monica Lewinsky affair and its political and moral implications. Quebert is deliberately provocative in eschewing an academic and clinical analysis of the situation and speaking in a chatty and intimate way about it, using the everyday language of the street. He speculates on how many Americans indulge in the form of sex that Clinton enjoyed with the young White House intern. Outrageously, he asks his student audience if they'd like to reveal their experiences. Not surprisingly, they studiously examine the floor. Except for Goldman, who recognises that his moment has come.

Standing on his chair, Marcus Goldman announces to the assembled company that he 'loves getting his dick sucked just like the President' and calls for God's blessing on the President, sex and America. Things happen quickly for Goldman after this: following the lecture he sells fifty copies of the college magazine which features one of his short stories, ten girls give him their telephone number, and he gets to meet Quebert, who later becomes a friend and adviser. He's also summoned to the Dean of Humanity's office to explain the meaning of his obscene behaviour in the morning's lecture. Goldman gives a chirpy re-run of his performance and tries to sell an apoplectic Dean a copy of the college magazine at its newly-inflated price.

It's all quite ludicrous and yet, like all good satire, it has parallels in real life: when asked what made him attract attention in the way he did, Goldman asserts that whilst 'sex can cause your downfall…. it can also propel you to the top'. And that's difficult to deny, given the example of those TV 'celebrities' whose rise to fame is attributable in no small measure to a carefully cultivated image based on the repeated use of four-letter words, sexual innuendos, or an exaggerated caricature of their sexual persuasion. Monica Lewinsky also did very well out of her revelations. Again, the seemingly farcical exchanges between Marcus and the Dean of Humanities have their parallels in real life and are very reminiscent of the famous

1960 Trial of *Lady Chatterley's Lover*, in which representatives of two entirely different cultures debated the meaning of 'obscenity' and demonstrated their complete inability to understand what the other was talking about.

The sexual revolution that took place in the second half of the 20th century not only changed many people's behaviour but also had a major impact on the way in which we now talk and write about sex. Penguin Books' successful defence of D H Lawrence's notorious novel as a genuine literary work gave authors the freedom to write explicitly on this subject, in language that had previously been widely used in real life but forbidden in print. Many taboos have been swept away and literature can now hold up a mirror to what goes on in the bedroom with an honesty that was denied writers in the past. Explicit sex has become an increasingly familiar feature of the novel in the last 50 or so years and some writers reel out free-standing and gratuitous sex scenes without any warning or preparation: eyes meet across a crowded room and a couple are smitten with a smouldering passion that must be consummated at the earliest opportunity.

I recently came across the works of the American novelist James Salter, or more specifically his *Light Years*, in which he presents a slice of life similar to that portrayed in F Scott Fitzgerald's *The Great Gatsby*. Vivi and Nebra Berland are members of a hedonist and bon vivant set that share various cultural interests and engage in witty and entertaining analysis of the human search for happiness. The men are strikingly handsome, the women beautiful and vivacious. Reasonably affluent and seemingly endowed with generous leisure time, these people appear to have it all. But they always want more: newer and more intense experiences.

Vivi and Nedra are happily married with two delightful daughters, but they are both engaged in passionate no-holds-barred affairs. In one relationship the mistress lays herself out enticingly, clearly inviting the man to do what he wishes with her. In the other, it is the man who fulfils the role of ideal partner. Judging her responses and controlling his movements within her to perfection, he enables his mistress to experience sustained and multiple orgasms, accompanied by wild screams of unimaginable ecstasy. It's sophisticated pornography, very well written and shockingly titillating. But the whole lifestyle and experience of the characters in *Light Years* is, as the book's title perhaps suggests, as far removed from reality as the fantasy worlds of Tolkien, Rushdie and J K Rowling.

John Updike's *Couples* puts James Salter's *Light Years* into perspective. Updike, best known for his 'Rabbit Angstrom' novels, is a sensitive and perceptive writer, skilled in revealing the hidden agendas of social and sexual relationships and the different perceptions that people have of the same situation. In *Couples* the intense excitement of the sexual act is certainly explicit, but so too are the frustrations. The book is an honest appraisal of the pain and pleasure of the love relationship and the lure and corrosive effect of adultery. It's both entertaining and thought-provoking.

6.

The Author's Passion

Jill and I are in the Lake District for a few days, staying in Grange-in-Borrowdale, a compact hamlet nestling in a vibrant green valley surrounded by sheep-grazing meadows with mountains rising above them on all sides. We were last here in 1958 and nothing appears to have changed in the intervening years. I am reminded of the sense of permanence induced by another beautiful scene described in the opening to Alan Paton's *Cry the Beloved Country*, a novel that I first read over 50 years ago. Paton describes the lovely African Valley of the *Umzimkulu* on its journey from the Drakensberg escarpment to the sea. But he warns that this fairest of valleys is vulnerable, its timeless quality fragile:

> "It is well tended, and not too many cattle feed upon it ; not too many fires burn it, laying bare the soil. Stand unshod upon it, for the ground is holy, being even as it came from the Creator. Keep it, guard it, care for it, for it keeps men, guards men, cares for men. Destroy it and man is destroyed."

In a few short sentences Paton has made us aware of his passion for his homeland and the importance he attaches to our understanding the interdependence of Man and the land on which he lives.

At its simplest level, the setting of a novel provides a context for the characters and action, a place the reader can visualise. But it's usually much more complex than that: our environment helps to shape our lifestyle and daily routine, the kind of problems we face and the decisions we take. So it is in a novel: the setting can be a significant player in the action. This is particularly so in a work like *Cry the Beloved Country* where it is fundamental to one of the key themes explored by an author driven by a deep love for his birthplace.

I have a Welsh friend who made his home in England but who became so frustrated by the loss of his Welsh connections that, at the age of 50, he set about learning the Welsh language. Upon retirement, Gareth Thomas moved back to Wales with his Polish wife and has subsequently had two novels published – first in Welsh and then in English. *A Welsh Dawn* is a love story, both personal and national, set against the political tensions of the 1950s. It's a very well-researched presentation of some of the difficulties the Welsh people have experienced in trying to establish and maintain their country's identity in the face of English domination. His second book, *I,Iolo*, is the story of a fascinating and enigmatic character called Edward Williams (1747-1826), better known by his bardic name Iolo Morganwg, who has a special, if controversial, place in Welsh history. Iolo was a leading collector of and expert on Medieval Welsh Literature and regarded by many as having made a lasting impact on Welsh culture, most notably for his founding of the Gorsedd of Bards which proclaims each National Eisteddford and conducts its major ceremonies Others, however, revile the bard for being a con man, forger and drug addict. Gareth identifies with his central character's fierce patriotism and tells his story through Iolo's own eyes. It's a most unusual and strangely entertaining novel, quite unlike anything else I've read.

Passion is at the heart of so many novels – passion for a place, person, cause, or just a better, fairer, kinder world. Perennially popular subjects with writers and readers are the great examples of man's inhumanity to man – apartheid, the slave trade, the holocaust, the two twentieth century world wars. Novelists return to these topics time and time again, with new insights, perceptions and compassion. It's just as well they do. Without this literary preoccupation, and the willingness of readers to face up to the harrowing details of brutal oppression, these momentous events might well dim in the memories of the general public and become the concern only of historians and researchers. The implications of that scenario don't bear contemplation.

The interest that novelists have in reminding us of the depths of human cruelty and depravity is not wholly driven by altruism, a burning desire to add their voice to those who try to build a better world. That is normally an important factor, but authors are also, of course, well aware that persecution, victimisation, corruption and all the other evil consequences of the abuse of power provide a rich source of tension and drama for their story-telling. The striving of lovers, friends and families to connect and forge meaningful relationships is heightened when countries are torn apart by internal conflict and civil war. The human desire for self-expression, personal development and freedom is deepened when totalitarian governments seek to subject their people to unquestioning obedience to their will. The memories authors have of their childhood have a special piquancy if the place in which they grew up has been ravaged by war.

Markus Zusac's *The Book Thief,* one of the novels with a surreal element mentioned in chapter 5, is set in Germany during the Holocaust and the Second World War. It tells of the incredible bravery and resilience of ordinary people who are true to themselves and each other in a time of extreme persecution and hardship. It's a powerful and moving story of love, friendship and loyalty, intensified by its setting. Extreme hardship, cruelty, victimisation and the arbitrary threat of death are ever-present, and yet the story is told with admirable restraint. The over-riding message is one of hope and faith in human courage, kindness and resilience.

Recent years have seen a spate of new novelists emerge from countries in which people's daily lives are lived amidst political turmoil and conflict. They give us an insider view of countries of which most of us have little knowledge or understanding beyond the news headlines. Ahdaf Soueif's *The Map of Love* is a story of love and friendship set in Egypt against a turbulent political background that provides disturbing insights into the effects of imperialism and its legacy in modern times. One of the key themes is the extent to which our lives are governed by the past actions of others. The author's love of her country is unmistakable and the exotic beauty of Egypt is a tangible force in the novel. There is a strong sense of history and of our ties to the land and our ancestors.

In the Country of Men is a first work by Hisham Matar, a young Libyan. The novel is set during the terror regime of Colonel Gaddafi who was ruthless in crushing any opposition. The story is told through the eyes of a nine-year-old boy,

Suleiman, whose father is a member of a protest group critical of the government and active in recruiting university students to its cause. Suleiman becomes aware of his father's activities from observing his parents' behaviour and overhearing scraps of conversation. The effect on his young life is dramatic and the reader identifies with his constant uncertainty and fear of violence. Suleiman's behaviour becomes increasingly disturbed as the family's routines are repeatedly disrupted. Violence breeds violence and Suleiman's reactions begin to mirror the cruelty that is being inflicted on those around him. Hisham Matar's novel presents an uncompromising picture of the way in which people act under extreme stress. It's one of a fast growing number of books that focus on the harsh realities of life in some Islamic countries.

A Thousand Splendid Suns by Khaled Hosseini, an Afghan who sought asylum in the United States, tells the story of two young women both married to a brutal and vindictive Kabul shoemaker in 21st century Afghanistan. It's an intensely painful story relieved only by the strength of character of the two women and the close friendship that develops between them as a result of their shared plight. There are similarities with Brian Keenan's *An Evil Cradling*, an autobiographical account of Brian Keenan's four years of savage treatment as the captive of fundamentalist Shi'ite militiamen in Lebanon. Both books are extremely disturbing, almost unbearable to read, yet ultimately uplifting and cathartic.

A Thousand Splendid Suns is a gripping story, fast-moving and yet detailed in its recounting of key incidents and their effect on the central characters. Hosseini knows just what to include in his narrative and what to leave to his readers' imagination. His method is episodic, the full picture being conveyed by the analysis of carefully-selected moments in the characters' lives. The effect of this alternating detail and pace in the narrative is to create suspense and anxiety regarding what is about to happen, none more so than when Laila's ex-boyfriend, Tariq, returns to Kabul several years after his alleged death and begins to visit Laila while her husband, Rasheed, is at work. The dangers of their meetings are obvious and we wait in fear of Rasheed's response to his young son's revelations about a stranger who has been entertained in his absence. The outward calm with which Rasheed receives this information is as dramatic and taut with the threat of violence as a Pinter play. I have rarely identified so strongly with the victims of cruelty and brutality as I did in this novel.

Even so, the Hosseini novel that made the biggest impression on me was the cleverly-crafted and beautifully written *And the Mountains Echoed*. It opens with a tragedy – the callous separation of two young siblings who have enjoyed a wonderfully close relationship. While we wait in the hope of a re-union, we move between different characters, countries and moments in time. The book's themes, however, remain constant as Hosseini explores the complex nature of kinship and friendship, human companionship and separation, allegiance and disloyalty, dependence and independence, selfishness and self-sacrifice, guilt and regret. The human dramas are played out against the background of recent events in Afghanistan and, as in *The Map of Love*, the strong relationship between the characters and their homeland is very evident. Hosseini cares deeply about his characters and writes most sensitively of the joys and sadnesses of their lives. I found it utterly convincing in its exploration of the nuances of human relationships and the emotional needs and fears that lead people to behave as they do.

The novelist, like the poet, is a tireless seeker after the universal and timeless truths of human existence. All genuine artists see the world around them with heightened sensitivity and seek to convey their impressions with a clarity and precision that deepen people's understanding of their own lives. Novelists describe imaginary situations and characters, which they then use to present their personally-observed view of life to their readers. Literature shines a light on the human situation and helps us to face up to what life has in store for us.

Markos Varvaris, one of the main characters in *And the Mountains Echoed*, recalls a conversation he'd had as a teenager with a young girl, Thalia, who had suffered an horrific accident in which a dog had ripped away most of her lower jaw. Thalia had lived with Markos's family and been like a sister to him. She'd had the chance to go to a prestigious private school and Markos had urged her to seize this opportunity. He'd told her that she was the smartest person he knew and that she'd be able to go to university and follow any career she wishes. She would become a scientist, a professor, an inventor. The 'thudding formality' with which Thalia had rejected this idea had brought the conversation to an abrupt end.

Many years later Markos trains as a plastic surgeon and understands something of which he'd been ignorant when he'd envisaged such a bright future for Thalia:

"I learned that the world didn't see the inside of you, that it didn't care a whit about the hopes and dreams and sorrows that lay masked by skin and bone. It was as simple, as absurd, and as cruel as that. My patients knew this. They saw much of what they were, would be, or could be hinged on the symmetry of their bone structure, the space between their eyes, their chin length, the tip projection of their nose, whether they had an ideal nasofrontal angle or not. Beauty is an enormous, unmerited gift given randomly, stupidly."

Observations like this are one of the great pleasures of reading, little nuggets of truth that sharpen your understanding of the human situation. Markos's reflections provide us with a further example as he contemplates the factors that led him to become a plastic surgeon:

"And so I chose my speciality to even out the odds for people like Thalia, to rectify, with each slice of my scalpel, an arbitrary injustice, to make a small stand against a world order I found disgraceful, one in which a dog's bite could rob a little girl of her future, make her an outcast, an object of scorn.

At least this is what I tell myself. I suppose there were other reasons that I chose plastic surgery. Money, for instance, prestige, social standing. To say I chose it solely because of Thalia is too simple – lovely as the idea may be – a bit too orderly and balanced. If I've learned anything in Kabul, it is that human behaviour is messy and unpredictable and unconcerned with convenient symmetries."

How tempting it is, despite the evidence to the contrary, to interpret something one hears or sees in a way that provides a neat solution to a problem, a coherent explanation, a balanced judgement. It used to be common practice for writers of fiction to draw all the threads of their narrative together in a concluding chapter that tied up loose ends and made a definitive statement on what happened to each character.

Modern writers are less concerned to strive for what Hosseini's character, Markos Vivaris, calls 'convenient symmetries'.

For many years I was an A level examiner, spending long summer evenings marking scripts after the day job of running a sixth-form college. Friends often asked me why I did it – after all, it's a tedious occupation, the pay is very poor, and you're working all the time under pressure to meet tight deadlines. The reward for me was coming across the occasional exceptional answer: I got a distinct buzz whenever a young student wrote really well, in denial of the constraints and artificiality of the exam situation.

I marked the paper that required students to give their response to two unseen passages, one a poem, the other a short piece of prose. Most candidates found this task really difficult and the academic rituals of literary criticism that they had been taught often proved more of a hindrance than a help, coming between the passages and the candidates' genuine thoughts about them. Thus a jargon-free answer that gave a truly personal response to each literary passage was a breath of fresh air. I threw caution to the winds with these exceptional answers and awarded them 21 or 22 marks out of 20 – on the grounds that they manifestly exceeded the highest standard that one could possibly expect an A level candidate to achieve under exam conditions. The subsequent anticipation of an audience with the chief examiner to explain myself added a little piquancy to the rest of my examining.

Among the many pleasures of reading literature are those moments in a book when we are struck forcibly by the universal truth of an author's observation, when we see something familiar in a completely different light, when the mundane becomes interesting, or the obscure is suddenly made comprehensible. Or we may delight in a description that brings a character or scene vividly to life, or a sudden unexpected twist in the plot that we haven't foreseen as a possibility, or the gradual building of anticipation or suspense. Or we detect undercurrents of feeling or meaning beneath the surface of a seemingly transparent conversation. But perhaps the greatest pleasure of all is when an author seems to be in direct contact with us, privy to our personal thoughts and feelings, and sharing confidences. Alan Bennett describes this author/reader relationship in his *Untold Stories*:

> "...the best moments in reading are when you come across something – a thought , a feeling, a way of looking at things – which you had thought unique and particular to you. Now here it is, set down by someone else, a person you have never met, someone even who is long dead. And it is as if a hand has come out and taken yours."

Bennett might have added that part of the pleasure of such occasions is often the eloquence with which your thoughts and feelings are being expressed – an eloquence that you feel you could not achieve yourself.

Whether intentionally or not, Alan Bennett constantly makes contact with his readers in the manner that he describes. He has a happy knack of locating, in his own life, impulses and experiences that others instinctively share. Bennett, with his trademark self-deprecating manner and dry wit, comes across as an ordinary bloke. His achievement is to make both his own and other people's ordinariness interesting. He takes the normal person's plebeian pleasures and mundane anxieties and turns them into a literary experience. If you read Bennett's stories and diaries you feel as if you know him: he's part of your life, which, I suppose, is why he's constantly referred to as 'a national treasure'.

One of the reading experiences that I particularly enjoy is when an author conveys the poignancy of a particular episode or scene in an image or description that exactly encapsulates the mood of the character or characters involved. Anne Tyler's *The Amateur Marriage* is the story of two teenage sweethearts who rush into a wartime marriage that proves increasingly difficult. The following passage describes Pauline's feelings when, after many years, her husband, Michael, finally leaves her:

> "Once again Michael hesitated, but then turned toward the foyer. She heard the latch, and a moment later his car lights lit up and he backed out of the driveway She went on staring straight ahead of her. She had a slippery off-balance feeling, the feeling that a person might get if she were sitting on a stopped train and the train next to hers started gliding away and she wasn't sure, for a second, whether it was her train or the other that was moving."

This is typical Ann Tyler. The life Pauline has known for so many years is slipping away from her and her feeling of disorientation is captured in a simple image with which we can immediately identify, a situation in which for a split second we fear we're losing touch with reality. It's a strange experience. I once drove along the road I normally took home from work to find that a long row of poplars in a field bordering the road had been felled during the day. Before I realised what had happened there was a moment almost of panic as I completely lost my bearings.

Loss is a recurring theme in fiction. Novels are much concerned with the inexorable passage of time and the constant fluctuations of fortune that determine the particular highs and lows that characterise most people's lives. Life is never static: we are always moving from one experience to another, leaving one stage of our life for the next. In the process we invariably feel a sense of loss at the point of transition, a feeling that intensifies as we grow older and cannot shut out our awareness of the transitory nature of our stay in this world. If there's a novel that doesn't deal at some point with the human sense of loss, in at least one of its many manifestations, then I cannot recall what it is. Coming of age; leaving one's birthplace; a missed opportunity; a new job or home; the ending of a friendship or love relationship; the death of someone close to us; sudden traumas, accidents, health issues that mean things will never be the same again – all these are a rich source of material for any writer who wants to tell it as it is.

Sue Miller's *The World Below* is a quiet, contemplative novel in which Catherine, the central character, discovers her grandmother's diaries and becomes absorbed in the life story they tell, so much so that it 'runs steady as a busy stream' underneath her own life. The idea of a 'world below' recurs throughout the novel in various guises and touches several of the characters. It relates to an incident in Catherine's childhood when she was taken out in a boat on a fascinating lake created by the damming of a river to form a reservoir. The area that had been flooded had included a sizeable settlement and, when the reservoir had been completed, some of the submerged buildings remained visible beneath the surface of the lake. Many years later, when she's a mother and grandmother, Catherine receives a letter from an old boyfriend that mentions this lake.

"It brought back to me suddenly the way the buildings had looked through the shifting mirror of the water, the way the world below was there and then not there and then there again, and the way I had felt that day looking down into it, dizzy with my sense of yearning and loss for what was gone, and somehow for all that ever would be gone, in my life."

It's a particularly poignant memory for Catherine, for her friend's letter recalls the occasion she'd told him about the lake and how the two of them had tried unsuccessfully to find the place she'd described seeing as a child. He'd been sceptical of her experience at the time but had recently read about the lake and visited it. Hence the letter – to apologise very belatedly for doubting her story many years ago. It had been a slight disagreement, but nonetheless hurtful to Catherine and the beginning of their relationship cooling and eventually ending. Many of our big changes of direction in life hinge on seemingly trivial matters and we are left wondering what would have happened had we reacted differently to a stray comment, a meaningful expression, a chance meeting.

7.

The Shared Pleasure of Reading

I've been very fortunate in my marriage to have a soul mate whose enjoyment of reading and discussing books matches my own. It adds significantly to the pleasure of a hobby or interest when there's someone with whom you can share your enthusiasm. It's a bonus that Jill and I also enjoy many of the same novels and writers – although our responses to them are sufficiently different to ensure that we're not merely endorsing each other's judgements.

Jill reads more biographies and autobiographies than I do, and this interest extends to the biographical details of fictional characters. I'm more likely than she is to revert to the established classics from time to time, but that's only because I have more gaps to fill, as she was an avid reader long before I developed the habit. She was the first person with whom I discussed books and a significant influence on my becoming a reader.

Jill attributes her early love of literature partly to her home background. Her mother lost much of her schooling because of illness and left school at 13. She married at 18 and quickly had three children. She was, however, a gifted young woman, responsive to music, drama and literature. She read to the children and Jill particularly remembers *Peter Pan, The Water Babies, Tom Sawyer, Oliver Twist,* and selected passages from *A Christmas Carol* and *Alice's Adventures in Wonderland.* It's perhaps worth noting that, despite his learning difficulties, Jill's brother Philip became a keen reader, and getting him to talk about his latest family or animal story was one of the ways in which we were able to coax him out of his normal silence.

The only overlap Jill and I appear to have had in our childhood reading was the *Girls' Crystal* paper, but, without an equivalent to the newspaper-delivery income that funded my extensive purchasing of comics, Jill was entirely dependent on tatty copies that had done the rounds. She also made a much earlier start on reading full-length storybooks than I did – some of Enid Blyton's *Famous Five,* but mostly the very popular Chalet Stories. In today's world the term 'chalet girls' conjures up lurid accounts of the sexual experiences of the young hostesses who work in European ski resorts, but in the 1940s it referred to a fictitious group of pupils attending an eminently respectable independent girls' boarding school. The *Chalet School* was the setting for a series of some sixty novels written by Elinor M Brent-Dyer. An oft-repeated story-line concerned the arrival of a disruptive or troubled newcomer who, with the support of her teachers and better-adjusted classmates, became a model pupil.

Jill quickly moved on to the great romances and other well-known classics. She remembers her first adult novel, *Silas Marner,* with great affection. Other early and happy memories are of *Black Beauty, Little Women, The Children of the New Forest* and, later on, *The Mill on the Floss.* At the age of 13, she began a friendship that had a significant influence on her reading. Jill and Eileen's friendship had a competitive edge to it – two classmates vying all the time for top marks. But it was also a close companionship fostered by the girls' fast-developing interest in some of the great heroines of English literature – Jane Eyre, Lorna Doone, Elizabeth Bennett, Rebecca, Tess, *Middlemarch's* Dorothea. The books were borrowed, shared and discussed at length. By her late teens Jill had read much of Jane Austen, Thomas Hardy and D H Lawrence. She didn't enjoy some of her prescribed school texts, such as Scott's *Ivanhoe*, and rejected Virginia Woolf's *To the Lighthouse*. In her early twenties she and two other young teachers rented a furnished flat whose owner's library was at their disposal. The Russian novels became a big attraction – first Dostoevsky and Turgenev, and then Tolstoy and Pasternak.

Jill and I feel that our main pleasure in life has come from our relationships – with each other, our family, our friends and, as educationists, the teachers with whom we've worked and the children and students we've taught. Nothing very remarkable about that, but we both realise how significantly this factor colours so much of what we do, how we prioritise our time and how we spend our money.

Our choice of reading material inevitably reflects our outlook and lifestyle. We both like family sagas and books about human relationships of every kind. The characters are crucially important : we must believe in and empathise with them. They don't have to be likeable, but we need to understand where they're coming from and why they behave as they do. We are interested in the different ways authors deal with the big events in people's lives – birth and death, coming of age, courtship and marriage, the moments of bonding and separation, the times of joy and tragedy. We respond to authors who provide new insights into the human predicament and stories of people's resilience in the face of adversity. Of course, ideally we look, too, for a good story, a clever and convincing plot and an author with a distinctive and attractive style. And Jill would add to that list 'an unusual or original setting', in fact would put that as a joint first requirement along with 'interesting and credible characters'. This marks a slight difference of emphasis in what we each look for in a book.

Two modern authors whom Jill has particularly enjoyed are Tracy Chevalier and Sebastian Faulks 'because they open up new vistas and explore a range of different settings for their novels'. This is an interesting pairing, as Chevalier and Faulks have both succeeded in bridging the gap between literary fiction and its popular and commercially-successful counterpart. It's quite an achievement to win the acclaim of both the general public and the literary critics. It's too easy to classify books as either popular page-turners (and so second-rate) or literature (thus respectable).

Both Tracy Chevalier and Sebastian Faulks write historical novels, Chevalier exclusively so. This is an added attraction for Jill, who has always taken a scholarly interest in other places and peoples, including past cultures and key historical events. She has a great love of learning and I have never been able to keep up with her wide-ranging curiosity about the world.

Jill and I came to Tracy Chevalier's novels via the usual route of her best known work, *The Girl with the Pearl Earring,* in which the author imagines the circumstances in which the celebrated Vermeer painting might have been produced and the role of the girl who inspired it. The descriptions of the Vermeer household and the town of Delft give a clear picture of what it was like to live in 17th century Holland, particularly for the servant class. We are, for example, made very conscious of the accidents and dangers to which working people were exposed in their daily lives at that time. The characters, too, have a very strong physical presence – their body language, the distinctive features and qualities of their voices and facial expressions, their sexuality, the physical discomfort and pain they experience, and their silent but often eloquent comings and goings.

In *Burning Bright,* Chevalier switches to late 18th century London at the time of the visionary poet, William Blake, who features in the story. Again, both the place and the characters are brought vividly to life and we experience the setting and the people so strongly through our senses that there is a real feeling of emptiness and loss when the book comes to an end.

In both *The Girl with the Pearl Earring* and *Burning Bright,* Tracy Chevalier recounts an extraordinary relationship between apparent opposites. In the first book, Griet, who becomes the famous painter's assistant and inspiration, is a lowly servant girl in the Vermeer household. In the second novel, there is a double juxtaposition of opposites, firstly between a country boy whose family have just arrived in London and a streetwise girl who becomes his guide and companion, and secondly between the two youngsters and a neighbour, William Blake, who develops a fatherly interest in them. A recurring theme in *Burning Bright* is the nature of innocence and experience, the subject of Blake's best known poems.

Contrasting characters also feature in Chevalier's *Falling Angels* which tells of the coming together of two very different families who are greatly affected by a shared tragedy. Daughters from the families develop a friendship with each other and with a young apprentice grave-digger in the fashionable Victorian graveyard which becomes the young friends' meeting place. It's a story of childhood friendship, sexual awakening and human vulnerability, set at the beginning of the 20th century. *Falling Angels* touches on a number of key issues of the time as England moves out of the Victorian era and begins to question well-established assumptions, particularly those relating to the role of women. Rich in historical detail and full of atmosphere, the story is told by the various characters in turn so that we see the events and their setting from different angles. This sharing of the narration throws the characters into strong relief, sharpening our awareness of their strengths and weaknesses, their prejudices, idiosyncrasies and beliefs.

I am inclined to think that my appreciation of the importance of a novel's setting has increased over the years, or perhaps it's just that this aspect of a writer's art has, with time, become much more skilful and sophisticated. But then both these possibilities are challenged by my recollection of how strong an impression Hardy's Wessex made upon me when I first read his novels over 60 years ago. I'm sure my love of Dorset owes something to that literary experience. Whatever importance a reader attaches to a novel's setting, it would be a particularly insensitive person who wasn't transported back into the past by Tracy Chevalier's historical novels. In the three books just mentioned she has, of course, chosen places and periods rich in descriptive opportunities. However, that's not true of all her novels.

At the Edge of the Orchard concerns a hard-working second-generation American family struggling to establish an apple orchard in the inhospitable swamplands of 19th century Ohio. The potential of the setting isn't obvious and yet the details of the farming background are completely absorbing. The apple-producing enterprise has two parts. James Goodenough's specialism is the nurturing of a sweet eating apple by painstaking grafting from an English Golden Pippin. His wife, Sadie, is more interested in the growing of 'spitters', a sour apple good for making cider (to which she is very partial). It's another significant contrast: the two different parts of the business are a cause of friction between husband and wife and their preference of apple symbolises their very different personalities, James gentle and sweet-tempered, Sadie sharp and spiky.

Tracy Chevalier's research into the art of apple-growing is meticulous and the first part of the novel is full of the aroma, taste and physical presence of the two species of apple that play an important part in the narrative. The story and its setting shift in the second part of the book, which follows the fortunes of Robert, the youngest son, after he has left home, following a tragic event on the farm. Robert works with trees, the giant redwoods and spectacular sequoias of California. He derives a peace from his relationship with these very special showpieces of nature which gives him respite from the inner turmoil that he experiences as a result of the tragedy that caused him to desert his family. Chevalier's research into the detail of her setting is once more very impressive and underpins an important theme in the novel that it shares with Alan Paton's *Cry the Beloved Country* – the extent to which Man should interfere with nature. The carefully-thought-out structure of *At the Edge of the Orchard* is a reminder of the craftsmanship that goes into a good novel. Chevalier is particularly skilful in the way in which she works real-life figures into her narrative

– the pioneering apple farmer and American folk hero, Johnny Appleseed, and the British plant collector, William Lobb.

The historical novels of Sebastian Faulks, another of Jill's favourite authors, include a trilogy of very different stories in distinctive settings, loosely connected by their French location and the way in which they show the effect of war on people's characters and lives. One of the characters, Charles Hartmann, appears in all three books.

The Girl at the Lion D'Or is a love story set against the background of the political instability of France in the 1930s. Anne Louvert, the girl of the book's title, has a shadow in her life cast by her father's execution during the First World War for alleged mutiny, and her family's subsequent disgrace and persecution as traitors.

Birdsong focuses on two characters living at different times: Stephen Wraysford, a British soldier fighting on the front line at Amiens in the First World War, and his granddaughter, Elizabeth Benson, who in the 1970s tries to acquire an understanding of his military experiences. The novel shows the devastating effects of trauma on people's lives and highlights the importance of recording the horrors of war for future generations.

Charlotte Gray is the most complex of the trilogy and deals with themes of memory and loss, love and death, resistance and capitulation at times of oppression. Charlotte, the central character, is a young British woman working for the French Resistance Movement during the Second World War. She becomes involved in helping Jewish families threatened by the Vichy Government's compliance with German demands for it to meet targets for deporting Jews to Drancy, a holding centre for Auschwitz. The scenes at both infamous camps are extremely harrowing. All three novels are painfully explicit in their descriptions of the precise nature of twentieth century military conflict and its disastrous consequences. The trilogy stands alongside Ian McEwan's *Atonement* and Pat Barker's *Regeneration Trilogy* as an unequivocal condemnation of war.

Sebastian Faulks is a good example of a writer well known for a particular interest who nevertheless ranges widely in the settings of his novels. *A Week in December* provides a marked contrast to the histories, focusing on some of the more irritating and unpleasant features of today's society. Faulks masters the satirist's art of taking a well-known aberration and pushing it just a little bit further than the reality. Among the targets are the various TV programmes in which members of the public are given a moment of glory by the media, but in the process often have their limitations and emotions cruelly exposed. In the reality show featured in *A Week in December* seriously ill people, suffering from dementia, schizophrenia, clinical depression etc, compete for a prize that will give them private treatment for their condition in a 'top hospital' for a year. A panel of judges urges the contestants on and sets them 'therapeutic challenges', such as trying to go two days without their medication. Ostensibly supportive, the programme, like its real-life equivalents, is quick to exploit human frailty for purposes of entertainment. In *A Week in December*, Faulks' satire ranges widely across a whole range of absurd and corrupt practices that constantly exploit the vulnerability of ordinary people. It penetrates beyond the humour that we normally associate with satire and exposes the extent to which we are culpable in our reluctance to protest or complain.

Engleby is another complete change. It's the life story of an oddball character, intelligent and able, but a loner and social failure. Engleby tells his own story and his keen insight into human affectations and foibles makes him an entertaining narrator. Despite a distinctly unpleasant side to his character, we find ourselves identifying with him. Our sympathy has been won over in the first part of the book which tells of the sickening bullying he habitually received at a third-rate public school where, as a scholarship boy from an ordinary home, he was regarded as an outsider. Faulks only gradually reveals what a frighteningly disturbed person Engleby is – by which time the reader has acquired the sort of understanding and compassion for him that one might have for a close relative suffering from a psychological disorder. There are echoes here of Lionel Shriver's *We Need to Talk about Kevin,* but I found I got inside Engleby's mind in a way that I didn't succeed in doing with Kevin.

Sebastian Faulks is much interested in mental disorder and the world of the psychiatrist. *Where My Heart Used to Beat*, another life-story, includes a lengthy discussion on the difficulties the medical profession has in understanding mental illness. *Human Traces* features two very able and ambitious medics who share a passion to understand the functions and malfunctions of the human mind. They form an alliance to find a cure for various forms of insanity. It's a complex and ambitious novel that combines a detailed survey of early psychiatry with a compelling narrative about human aspirations and relationships. A key episode that severely tests the strength of the consultants' friendship and professional partnership involves a difference of opinion over whether one of their patients has a purely physical condition or one caused by a traumatic experience.

Faulks' novels are tailor-made for Jill – great variety, but also a number of particular interests that are looked at from different angles and in different settings. Although a generalist in her search for knowledge, Jill responds readily to opportunities to look at a subject in more depth. She would have made an excellent researcher, had life taken her in that direction. And she'd have experienced few of my reservations about academia: she'd have loved it.

Jill's schoolteachers automatically assumed she would go to university, but responsibilities at home – care of her mother during a lengthy illness and also of a four-year-old sister and handicapped teenage brother at the same time – meant that she missed most of her sixth-form studies and never sat her exams. Homerton Teachers' Training College gave her a place on her headteacher's recommendation and her academic potential became very apparent there.

On completion of her teacher-training course, Jill had the chance to go on to King's College London to study theology but, conscious of the sacrifices her parents had already made to enable her to proceed to higher education, she opted to become a wage-earner. Such decisions were not uncommon at that time and Jill has never expressed regret at a missed opportunity. She would say that, in supporting her husband and children in their studies and university careers, she has had a vicarious academic experience that has been one of the rewards for the care role she has chosen throughout her life. That doesn't lessen our awareness of the enormous debt we owe her.

A short while ago Jill read *The Narrow Road to the Deep North* by the Tasmanian writer, Richard Flanagan, whose father had been a prisoner-of-war on the infamous Burma

Railway built with forced labour by the Japanese in the Second World War. The novel captures the incredible courage of the prisoners in the face of the most brutal and sadistic treatment by their Japanese captors. It was a new setting for Jill and when she'd finished the book she turned straight away to *The Railway Man* by Eric Lomax, who was himself a POW working on the notorious railway. There have been other occasions when Jill has been keen to follow up a book that she's found very interesting with another novel on the same, or a similar, subject. For example, *The Cellist of Sarajevo,* Steven Galloway's fictionalised account of the 1992-6 siege of Sarajevo, led directly on to Helen Dunmore's novel, *The Siege*, which deals with the 900-day bombardment of Leningrad during the Second World War.

I frequently read successive novels by the same author, but am not inclined to explore a particular subject in this concentrated way. I'd certainly never think of doing so after reading a war story such as *The Narrow Road to the Deep North* or *The Cellist of Sarajevo*. I have to pace myself over vivid accounts of Man's inhumanity to Man: I can only take so much at a time.

Fictionalised accounts of oppression, brutality and cruelty can be more powerful than the media reports of their real-life equivalents. Harrowing as the daily newspaper and TV coverage of human suffering is, it tends to be universal, generalised and repetitive, so that the reader and viewer build up an immunity to it. Novelists break through that defence by presenting particularised instances of human misery. When we empathise with their characters, we begin to feel that we know them personally and their plight moves us to compassion for the human race.

Novels trace the events that lead to tragedy and take us behind doors that are closed to journalists and photographers. We see the persecution, brutality and cruelty as they are enacted, not just the consequences that provide the scenes normally covered by the news bulletins. No account of asylum seekers' experiences travelling from their home country to the United Kingdom has moved me as much as the story of Farouk's ill-fated journey in Donal Ryan's *From a Low and Quiet Sea*. The opportunity that novelists have to arouse our compassion gives them a very powerful voice of protest against corruption, injustice and the violation of human rights. That, of course, is why they are so frequently criminalised in totalitarian states.

In real life you can't get inside another person's mind to the extent that you often do with a character in a good book. However, lifetime partners can have a good shot at it. Jill and I are reasonably confident that, if one of us enjoys a book, the other is also likely to do so. But we can sense when that assumption may be questionable and we'll occasionally issue a warning that there may be some side-effects to take into account with regard to the particular book that we're soon going to be passing on. Jill is very aware of my 'small doses' approach to horrific war scenes and detailed accounts of the abuse of power. And she's both understanding and protective. She's much more stoical than I am over tough content, although she did question the heavy emphasis on sexual perversity in Elizabeth Strout's 2017 *Anything is Possible*.

Preferences in reading are a very individual matter, reflecting as they do a person's character, lifestyle and past experiences. I'm fairly confident that I can choose an appropriate book for Jill or one of our three children, but after that I'm cautious. When buying books for members of the extended family I usually consult the person who best knows them before making my purchase. I'm similarly hesitant over suggesting titles that other people might like. The books I've mentioned in this reading memoir aren't intended to be recommendations: they're simply examples of the kind of novels that I enjoy, with some indication of why I chose them and how I reacted to them. Of course, I have a sneaky hope that readers might be tempted to try one or two of the novels I mention that they don't know and subsequently share my enjoyment of them, but I'm not banking on it. The pleasure one gets from reading is such a personal thing.

Just occasionally I'm so impressed by a novel I've read that I abandon my normal caution and recommend it warmly to all and sundry. Some years ago I reacted to a book in a way that I had never done before and have never done since: on finishing it I immediately turned back to the first page and started reading it a second time. The book was Arundhati Roy's *The God of Small Things* and, uncannily, Jill responded in precisely the same way. Again, she'd never done that before and hasn't since. I didn't seek feedback from those to whom I recommended Arundhati's outstanding novel, but I did receive unsolicited reactions from two people who tried it and 'couldn't get on with it'. Very salutary.

Another book that I couldn't prevent myself enthusing over to friends and relations was John Williams' *Stoner*, but then the world and its dog were recommending this novel at the time that I read it. *Stoner* is a phenomenon. Published in 1965, it had respectful and respectable reviews, sold quite well (just under 2000 copies), and eventually went out of print – a familiar pattern. However, enthusiasts, among them a number of famous authors, continued to talk and write about it and keep it alive through the decades. It was re-issued several times and sales justified the reprints. In 2011 a French translation sold really well and then it suddenly took off in this country. Julian Barnes named it 'the must-read novel of 2013'; it was Waterstone's Book of the Year; and Ian McEwan sang its praises on the BBC's Today Programme. In the second half of 2013 it sold 140,000 copies. Novels are often re-vitalised as a result of an author's gaining a prestigious award such as the Nobel Prize or because a successful film version appears, but there was no such spur for *Stoner*. Its amazing re-birth seems purely the result of word-of-mouth recommendations, and particularly those of loyal fellow-writers.

The response to *Stoner* has always been rather less positive in Williams' own country than in Europe. Tim Kreider, writing in the *New Yorker*, attributes this to America's being 'the land of dreams'. He contrasts John Williams' book with the revered American Classic, *The Great Gatsby*. Despite Gatsby's delusions and bad end, Americans think he's pretty cool: "He makes a mint of money, looks like a million bucks, owns a mansion, throws great parties, and even gets his dream girl, for a little while, at least." The contrast with the very unheroic Stoner couldn't be greater. It all comes down to what you look for in a novel – escapism or reality.

8.

Children's Potential to Become Lifelong Readers

Some years ago Jill and I visited Blackwell House in Cumbria, one of the best preserved and interesting of the Country's arts and crafts houses. Among the many fascinating artefacts and exhibits was one that had nothing to do with the origins of the house at the time of the Arts and Crafts Movement. It was a notebook in which visitors who had been members of the junior department of Huyton College had recorded their memories of their evacuation to Blackwell House for the duration of the Second World War air-raids on Liverpool. The book was full of happy memories of the educational opportunities the girls had enjoyed – in idyllic surroundings and under the guidance of their enlightened headteacher, Miss Murphy. The ex-pupils recalled their fell walks, the camps they were allowed to build in the woods, the conversion of the main hall of the house into a gymnasium, and the flooding of the courtyard during the winter to provide a skating rink. They remembered their swimming lessons in Lake Windermere wearing rubber rings attached by ropes to Miss Murphy, their midnight abseiling in pyjamas down the outside of the house as part of the school's fire drill, and the nightly bedtime routine when Miss Murphy read to the whole dormitory.

Jill's happy memories of her own bedtime stories ensured that the last thing she did before tucking our children up in bed was to read to them. She was a very good reader, employing a wide range of dramatic voices, including those of all the farmyard characters. If I was home from work in time I was able to take a share in the reading. I particularly remember the bear books which told of the adventures of a variety of ursine characters – Rupert, Pooh, Paddington and Little Bear. My favourite was a collection of Little Bear stories written by Else Holmelund and enhanced with delightful drawings by the American illustrator, Maurice Sendak, best known for his story picture book, *Where the Wild Things Are*. The series focuses on the interaction between Little Bear, a small cub, and his mother, Mother Bear, and on his yearning for his father, who is a ship's captain and away from home for long periods of time.

Little Bear is a loveable and rather wistful little chap who enjoys a very good relationship with his mother. He's quite an adventurous and imaginative young fellow and one day he makes himself a space helmet out of a cardboard box. It has two splendid earflaps and two pieces of wire for antennae. 'I'm going to fly to the Moon,' he informs Mother Bear. She expresses doubts that such an expedition is achievable by a fat little bear with no wings or feathers.

Little Bear is undeterred and sets off up a hill, climbs up a small tree and then jumps into the air. Predictably he lands with a bump and rolls down the hill. Taking stock of his surroundings, he concludes that the Moon looks very like the earth. He comes to a house that reminds him very much of his own home. Going in, he discovers lunch is served. A Mother Bear enters and exclaims at the sight of the visitor. 'Are you a bear from Earth?' she asks. 'Yes, I am,' says Little Bear. Mother Bear explains that she had a Little Bear, but he has left the Moon and flown to Earth, so her unexpected guest can have her Little Bear's lunch.

> "Little Bear put his arms around Mother Bear. He said, 'Mother Bear, stop teasing. You are my Mother Bear and I am your Little Bear, and we are on Earth, and you know it. Now may I eat my lunch?'
>
> 'Yes,' said Mother Bear, 'and then you will have your nap. For you are my Little Bear and I know it.' "

The point at which Little Bear feels that it's time to end playing 'make believe' and return to the security of the real world and his mother's arms is very poignant – a foretaste of those moments of great sensitivity and emotion that children will later encounter as adult readers of fiction.

One unexpected outcome of my participation in our family's nightly reading sessions was that I developed a modest talent at story-telling. Initially my stories were told to our eldest daughter and all of them involved her three bedmates – Teddy, floppy rabbit Dylan and their black friend who went under the extremely politically-incorrect name of Wogit. By the time the younger children got in on the act I had moved on to real-life characters. One particularly popular series featured a nun called Sister Charity who had strong connections with our local church and led weekly discussions that were often held in our house. She was a lively and jolly character who intrigued the children, particularly when she began to feature prominently in the bedtime story-telling.

I have always maintained that one of Sister Charity's distinctive features was that she went bare-footed, but I may be confusing the real person and my fictitious version. Certainly her lack of shoes was a crucial factor in the bed-time narratives in which she featured, for her remedy for sore and blistered feet was to flap her voluminous black habit and become airborne. She was a familiar sight circling above the village, looking for situations in which she would have a role to play. I think it added spice to the stories when they were told while Sister Charity was actually present in the house.

The demand for more 'flying Sister' stories seemed inexhaustible and eventually outran my imagination. I think Jill was actually quite relieved when the series came to an end: she admitted afterwards that, on occasions when the children had met the real life heroine of their bed-time stories, she'd been apprehensive that one of them might ask her about some of her airborne adventures. The experience left me with a healthy respect for writers who can keep coming up with new ideas for storylines about the same character or group of characters.

Our eldest grandson is Head of English in a secondary school, a comprehensive with a wide range of pupil attainment levels. The other day he asked me to name the greatest book ever written. I sensed this was an important test of my literary knowledge and one that I was going to fail. Sure enough, after a few attempts – the Bible, the Complete Shakespeare and some of the academics' favourites, such as *Ulysses* and the ubiquitous *Lord of the Rings*, I had to give up. 'It's *The Very Hungry Caterpillar*,' explained Tom. Apparently he's discussed his 'greatest book' question with all his classes. The answer is always the same: Eric Carle's story of a caterpillar who eats his way through a variety of foodstuffs before pupating and emerging as a butterfly. Nearly all children – avid readers, average readers , non-readers – can recall their great enjoyment of this book from their toddler days. Apparently it's sold over three million copies, the equivalent of one every minute since it was first published in 1969.

One of the joys of parenthood is observing the delight of little children in their first experiences of story-telling. Children are born with an intense desire to learn about themselves and the world around them and one of the ways in which this manifests itself is in their interest in reading and listening to stories. The challenge for parents and teachers is to foster this interest so that children experience a lifetime of enjoyment from the reading of literature.

As with all education, the pace and direction of the learning process needs to be determined by the child's interests, changing needs and capacity for learning. The adult's task is to create a supportive environment in which children maintain and develop their love of stories – sharing children's pleasure in the books they most enjoy, gradually widening their range of interest, making age-relevant books available in the home and in class libraries at school.

Enthusiasts for literature have to resist imposing their own tastes on children and introducing adult books too soon. Parents and teachers can sometimes be too impatient for progress in their management of the learning process, moving on from one stage to the next before children are ready. The habit of reading to children, for example, is often dropped early on in their development and is currently out of fashion in the secondary school where it is often deemed too leisurely and peripheral an activity in the present climate of cramming for national exams. Yet there is no age at which we outgrow the pleasure of listening to a good reader.

My strongest memory of being read to is from my university days at Birkbeck, a College that provided an opportunity for mature students to obtain an internal London University degree. The students on the English course were mostly in their late twenties and early thirties. Yet we didn't feel patronised when our professor read poetry to us. Professor Tillotson had a quiet, unremarkable voice, but he read with a wonderful sense of a poem's meaning – its nuances, rhythms and changes of pace. Every emphasis, pause and variation was given a precise weight. He didn't declaim or perform in any way, but allowed a poem to speak directly to us. It was a memorable experience.

The development of children's love of reading is a shared responsibility between the school and the home. And, ideally, there'll be constant communication between the two, with parents coming in to hear children read and joining staff and pupils for the various book events that schools organise – book club meetings, visits to libraries and exhibitions, authors reading and talking about their books. Some infant and primary schools invite parents in to hear books being read to a class, or in assembly, in the hope that this will be a stimulus to parents to develop the skills and confidence to read regularly to their children at home. Of course, this kind of liaison is an ideal to which some schools simply don't aspire. Many children come from homes in which books are a long way down the agenda, if indeed they feature at all. Schools serving areas of deprivation understandably often feel that they have little hope of encouraging parents to engage their child in desirable educational experiences such as reading for pleasure.

Initiatives to encourage children to read regularly are usually instinctive in the primary school. Far less so at the secondary stage. Here reading for pleasure is one of many important educational experiences that frequently get sidelined by the heavy emphasis on specialist academic studies leading to national exams. It's a short-sighted policy, not least because reading increases children's capacity to access knowledge and raise their performance level in their various academic subjects.

I've recently spent a good deal of time listening to young people talking about the pleasure of reading. It's made me very aware of the way in which children's reading habits change as they work their way through the formal education system. The following email I've just received is from a particularly keen reader, but the decline in time devoted to reading for pleasure follows a very common pattern:

"I can't remember when I first fell in love with reading – I remember being desperate to go to the 'big' library when I was in Year 2 and I think it grew from there. At primary school I read absolutely loads and pretty much anything – I had a lot of time to read and wasn't fussy about what it was. Some of the books/authors that stand out are The Famous Five, Malory Towers, Michael Morpurgo, Harry Potter, Cherub, The Roman Mysteries (I loved historical stories). I also remember reading some bigger reads such as Wild Swans (haven't read it since). The books that bridged the gap between young adult and adult were authors like Stephenie Meyer, Veronica Roth and Philip Pullman – I still love the Divergent series by Veronica.

Once I got to secondary school there was sadly much less time. I still got through a lot of books in the holidays and when I had time at school, but mostly easy reads, although definitely adult content by this point (I suppose I started to read adult novels pretty early, definitely by the end of primary school) – things like Tess Garritsen, James Patterson, John Green, Stieg Larsson, Dan Brown – mostly detective reads (seems to be the genre most written about!).

I read similar things now, any form of novel from the library likely to hold my interest for long enough, nothing particularly of note. I read a lot more textbooks and subject-related books now I'm studying at university, and sadly I don't really have much time to read for pleasure and, when I do, it's too much effort to read anything vaguely classical – hence I've never really read Jane Austen!''

A recurring theme in my most recent discussions on childhood reading experiences has been the negative impact of the secondary school approach to literature. Almost all GCSE students, regardless of whether they are likely to study English at university, or indeed to go to university at all, are put through a highly specialist course in university-style critical appreciation. At a time when they should be encouraged to extend their own reading as widely as possible, teenagers spend two years – and in some schools three – engaged in painstaking dissection of a very limited number of set texts. Here is a typical reaction to this process from a male undergraduate:

"The GCSE set books are chosen for you without any reference to the sort of thing 15 and 16-year-olds are likely to read and enjoy. That's a big problem.... I had no interest from the start. There was no personal involvement. I felt remote from the books we were reading....I'm quite a keen reader, but it wouldn't occur to me to read authors like Dickens and Jane Austen.... the Brontës or Thomas Hardy. The Shakespeare was really boring. It would have helped if we could have acted some of the scenes, but we just read the play like a novel."

The following comments from a prospective English specialist give, as one would expect, a different perspective:

"I found the set books hard at first. I had to keep going back over passages and looking up the meaning of words that I didn't know. Everyone found it difficult and this meant that the teacher had a lot of explaining to do. He did all the talking. There wasn't really much chance for people to take part. The teacher also had to tell us how we had to analyse literature and most students found this very boring. But I began to enjoy the analysing and to understand the books we were studying. I chose English as one of my A levels and want to study it at uni."

Despite her enthusiasm for the critical appreciation process, this student didn't feel that her GCSE course had influenced her general reading. She hadn't, for example, thought of extending her reading of authors to whom her English course had introduced her. This accorded with a general impression that studying literature at school is seen as a quite different activity from that of reading for pleasure.

Very few of the set texts traditionally prescribed for GCSE English Literature courses are enjoyed by students, but there are a small number of exceptions. One novel, in particular, has captured the imagination of generations of teenagers and had a similar effect on some of them to that which Hardy's *Mayor of Casterbridge* had on me many years ago. It's the American classic and 1960 Pulitzer prize-winner, *To Kill a Mocking Bird,* written by Harper Lee. It's an adult novel dealing with rape and racial inequality, but one that provides an excellent bridge between what one of the students I've quoted earlier in this chapter referred to as the gap between 'young adult' and 'adult' reading.

It's not difficult to see why Harper Lee's novel has survived its academic dissection in the classroom and become a book that many teenagers have actually enjoyed. It's a pacy, entertaining narrative full of incident and interesting characters. It's humorous and admirably accessible, but also constantly thought-provoking, contrasting the world as it is with how it could and should be. There's a mystery surrounding a young recluse who is imprisoned in his home by his parents and a highly dramatic court scene in which a negro is convicted of a rape that he didn't commit. In the key character, Atticus, the book has one of the great iconic literary heroes, a man of wisdom and great integrity who is also warm, down-to-earth and extremely likeable. *To Kill a Mocking Bird* is about prejudice and its opposites – tolerance, understanding and compassion. It doesn't preach, but it has a clear universal and timeless message about the difference between right and wrong. For what it's worth, it's top of my list of books that I feel every young person should have the opportunity to read before attaining adulthood.

American literary classics have served British readers well over the years and *To Kill a Mocking Bird* is not the only one to have found its way onto our school examination syllabuses. Steinbeck's *Of Mice and Men,* Maya Angelou's *I Know why the Caged Bird Sings* and Arthur Miller's play, *The Crucible,* are others. *Of Mice and Men* has been a particular favourite with the exam boards. It hasn't had the widespread seal of approval that teenagers have given to Harper Lee's novel but, if we must inflict a detailed university-style analysis of adult novels on all children, then Steinbeck's little masterpiece isn't a bad choice. For one thing it's short – 100 pages.

In an entry to a journal he kept, Steinbeck once noted that in all 'honest writing' there is a basic theme of people trying to understand one another. His hope for mankind, as it has been for Anne Tyler and many other writers, was that, if we can only understand each other, we will be kind to each other. Steinbeck worked for two years as an itinerant farm worker in the Salinas Valley, the part of California in which *Of Mice and Men* is set, and his two main characters are representative of the thousands of dispossessed and exploited farm workers in the American West during the 1930s. The novel is a universal parable about human loneliness, loss, friendship and hope. It tells the story of a close relationship between two labourers who drift from one farm job to another, sustained by a shared dream of one day owning their own land. The relationship between George and Lennie is special, in that Lennie has the mind of a young child so that, big and strong as he is, he's entirely dependent on George for guidance and protection. George complains constantly about the burden this places upon him, but he is unfailingly loyal to his vulnerable friend.

Character, setting and theme are all important in a Steinbeck novel; but so too is the narrative. *Of Mice and Men* was originally entitled *Something that Happened* and the book tells a powerful story based on an incident that Steinbeck witnessed in real life. We sense, as soon as we meet George and Lennie, that everything that happens to them has a significance in the story and, as the narrative builds to its dramatic climax, we are increasingly aware that it's heading for a tragic outcome. However, as in all good stories of suspense, the reader is kept guessing as to the exact nature of what is going to happen.

I have always understood the term 'English literature' to refer to works written in the English language. Our present Government has a different view – that it should apply only to works written by those of English (or, presumably, British) nationality. In the last 30 years our education system has changed from being one of the least to one of the most politically controlled in the world. As a consequence, each newly-elected government sets about changing the education system in accordance with its own political agenda. Worse still, successive Secretaries of State for Education, within the same government, introduce measures clearly based on their own personal prejudices. Michael Gove, appointed Secretary of State in 2010, carried this trend to a new level of interference by introducing a whole raft of changes in syllabuses and the way in which they are taught. In the process he declared his personal distaste for Steinbeck's *Of Mice and Men* and decreed that GCSE English Literature syllabuses should focus on 'home-grown' authors. Consequently, the four English exam boards have removed several of their most popular GCSE texts from the English literature syllabuses they offer. It has not escaped attention that the offending literary works were all written by fervent advocates of a more just, fair and compassionate society.

I am deeply concerned at the present level of political control of priorities and procedures that have always been the responsibility of experienced professional educationists and I have immense respect for teachers who still strive to implement their educational ideals, despite the context in which they now have to work. I'm also constantly impressed by the resilience of many young people who manage to retain their enthusiasm for learning in the present inhospitable educational climate. There are different ways of satisfying the desire to learn and many of those who are utterly frustrated by the Government's factory methods find other routes, some of them while they're still at school, others later on in adult life.

I have a very good ICT guru who rarely fails to sort out the manifold problems that I encounter in my attempts to achieve computer literacy. He was only 11 or 12 when he acquired this responsibility but he was a big improvement on the professional adult experts he replaced: he's more sensitive to my limited understanding and knowledge of the technical terms, and he moderates the pace of his advice accordingly. I asked him once, after he'd coaxed me through a particularly difficult problem, how he'd acquired his technical skills. 'Well', he said, 'I suppose I know my way around the computer. Whenever I have a problem, I try to work it out for myself. I try different things until I find the answer. And, because I've found it out for myself, I remember it.'

This independence in learning has stood my young consultant in very good stead, for he's dyslexic and finds the present educational methods completely at odds with the ways in which he learns. Dyslexic children – and there are many of them – find it very difficult to process letters and sounds. Consequently reading and writing are extremely slow and exhausting activities. In a system based on an assumption that everyone can, and should, be academically successful, dyslexic children are often thought to be unintelligent, lacking in concentration, or just not interested in learning. They are encouraged to work harder, given extra support, allowed more time to complete their work or exam answers. Well-meaning as these measures may be, they simply add to the time that these children spend struggling to master methods of learning that are completely inappropriate for them.

The progress achieved by this 'work harder' approach will always be slight and a poor return for the added pressure that children experience. A child's dyslexia won't go away. It needs to be understood, and those who experience it given the opportunity to concentrate on other ways of learning. Children with dyslexia have the same potential as other children to develop creative, practical, vocational and social skills. Their powers of reasoning and imagination are unimpaired. They can respond in the same way to visual stimuli and opportunities to express themselves orally. Given the opportunity to learn in ways other than the academic, they have the same chance as everyone else to make a success of their lives. In fact, freed from the burden of academia, they often forge ahead on creative, practical and vocational courses, appearing to have compensatory strengths in these areas.

My young ICT consultant talks to me about some of the alternative ways in which he learns, and gains pleasure from learning:

"At the age of about nine I became very interested in street dancing. I watched dancers on Facebook and Youtube for hours on end. I thought they were really cool. I began to choreograph my own dances and perform them in the school playground and to my family. That led me to join a dance class that had a street dancing group or crew. We entered competitions and gave public performances.

I wasn't particularly interested in the competitive side, but I got a great rush of adrenaline from the performing. I enjoyed expressing myself. I found dancing and performing gave me a tremendous release of energy and emotion. I enjoyed the idea of impressing people. I also liked adding dance, or whatever, to a character in the plays we used as a basis for the shows that we did. The combination of dance, drama and story-telling in general was very exciting and when I was 16 I enrolled for a BTEC Performing Arts course at a sixth-form college known for the wide range of courses it offered. I joined the group focusing on the various skills needed to perform in musicals. I don't read music, but I managed to pass grade 8 in jazz sax when I was 15. I'm learning to sing and I'm attending classes in ballet.

Some years ago I discovered the excitement of the theatre. In my GCSE course we were sat in rows of desks and had to study Shakespeare's *Macbeth*. Everyone found it a chore. Being made to learn something that doesn't interest you, and that your brain can't take in, never ends well. It gave me none of the pleasure I'd experienced in watching people perform and in performing myself. I just didn't get it. I learnt later in College that this way of looking at the play wasn't what Shakespeare intended. It was written to be performed, but in our studying of the play Shakespeare wasn't communicating with us. When we first read *Macbeth* in the classroom I wasn't intrigued and didn't understand why all this old English was so special.

Then months later when I'd started at College I went to see the play. I had no interest in any of Shakespeare's plays after studying one of them at school, and I wasn't planning on ever looking at *Macbeth* again. But my mate bought me a ticket and I said I'd go with him. He really wanted to see it, but I wasn't expecting anything.

I learnt so much that night. I was amazed . I thought it was incredible. And I understood completely what it was saying. Shakespeare's a genius.

Kids in school have a mindset about all education, as they should. They're told to learn and study stories, and that's not how it should be. You should be interested in stories and books and wanting to find out more about them. By giving kids Shakespeare at school and, more particularly, not presenting it in the correct context, you're giving them a false impression that they'll carry with them for years.

People will always learn from something they are truly curious about. Reading and viewing a play are two entirely different things. The exam courses have got it all wrong. Everyone enjoys learning. It's education that's the problem.''

9.

Small is Beautiful

Just occasionally, when a novel is failing to hold my attention fully, I recall a one-line review attributed to the American short-story writer and caustic critic, Ambrose Bierce: "The covers of this book are too far apart."

Bierce was obviously commenting on quality rather than actual length: good writers can sustain a reader's interest no matter how long it takes them to tell their story or make their point. Vikram Seth's *A Suitable Boy* is nearly 1500 pages long, but when I read it I didn't want it to come to an end. Jill is currently on a schedule of late nights, engrossed in Paul Auster's *4 3 2 1*. Its page count – a modest 860 – is deceptive, for the print is small, the lines close together and the book's dimensions like those of an encyclopaedia.

Having said this, I'm well aware that, given the choice between brevity and prolixity, I always go for the former. Many of the authors whose works I particularly enjoy, and have read in their entirety, favour the short novel format. Anita Brookner's and Penelope Lively's many novels average 200-250 pages in length and Edna O'Brien's considerably less. Many of Ian McEwan's are less than 200 pages long. William Trevor, Colm Toibin and Anne Tyler vary the length of their books slightly more, but average about 250-275 pages. Graham Swift and Sue Miller much the same.

The term 'novella' has been coined in recent years to describe particularly short novels, those that have 100 to about 150 pages. Most typically, they focus on a brief period during which the main character or characters experience a significant relationship or defining event that remains with them for the rest of their lives – a missed opportunity or unexpected change of circumstances, a heightened enjoyment of life, or a tragedy of some kind. Long novels cover a wide range of such situations; very short novels usually take just one and explore it in great detail.

William Maxwell's *So Long, See You Tomorrow,* for example, tells the stories of two sad and lonely young boys who form a fleeting friendship that is brought to an abrupt end when one of the companions moves away after traumatic events in his family. Fifty years later, the other boy recalls what happened, imagining the details that weren't recorded in newspapers at the time. He relives a situation of his own that had enabled him to empathise with his friend. His recollections are given an added poignancy by a regret that he has harboured all his life: not long after the tragedy that befell his friend he'd had an opportunity to renew contact but hadn't taken it.

So Long, See You Tomorrow is a heart-breaking study of human relationships and the effect on the young when adults mess up their lives and make irrevocable decisions without thinking of the consequences. Maxwell combines a wonderful evocation of a bygone age with a timeless portrayal of childhood and family life. There is a consistent ring of truth about this story that makes it special : you never feel that the characters are being manipulated for dramatic effect. The author has a sharp eye for the small details that reveal the nuances of human relationships and sow the seeds of change and disaster.

Susan Hill's *In the Springtime of the Year* is another novel permeated by a sense of loss. It's over 30 years ago that I read it but the memory of the impression it made on me remains very powerful. The book explores the feelings, memories and behaviour of a nineteen-year-old girl who loses her husband in an accident. It traces her grief from a state of complete inertia and withdrawal from human contact through to the early stages of her recovery.

Susan Hill returned to the theme of grief in the 2011 novella, *A Kind Man* – a parable about love and selflessness in which a young wife has to come to terms with the death of her three-year-old daughter and then the ill-health and death of her husband. The 'kind man' of the book's title is the young woman's husband, who acquires a divine gift – the ability to relieve pain and cure illness. It's a fast-moving and absorbing narrative that pressurises the reader to finish it at one sitting.

Susan Hill is a powerful and original story-teller, extremely sensitive to atmosphere, mood and the physical environment. She can portray a scene in a few significant brushstrokes. There is no gratuitous detail, no lengthy build-up to key incidents and little background information on the characters. The reader is not, for example, told in what period *A Kind Man* is set, but has no difficulty in working that out from the moving portrayal of poverty and joblessness.

Short novels usually concentrate on the emotional and psychological development of the characters and explore the complexity and contradictions of their response to a particular incident in their lives. The narrative tends to proceed in a straight line without twists and turns or changes of time or place. The plot is simple, sometimes virtually non-existent. The pace is often more leisurely than that to which we're accustomed in a conventional novel because the writer's canvas is much smaller, with far fewer events, characters and themes.

In *A Month in the Country,* by J L Carr, the gentle pace of the narrative is an essential part of the book's message and impact. Tom Birkin, back from the battlefields of the 1914-18 war, has been employed to uncover a mural thought to exist under coats of whitewash in a village church in the north of England. The repetitive and routine nature of his work, together with the peace and tranquillity of his surroundings, have a healing effect on him, after the horrific scenes he's witnessed at the front. The slow pace of rural life and the timeless landscape represent a country very gradually regaining its order and normality after a period of immense upheaval.

Tom is alone but not lonely. He forms a relationship with another survivor of the battlefield, working to discover a hidden grave in the churchyard. He meets some of the villagers and becomes friends with the vicar's wife, the attractive and slightly coquettish Alice, who is a frequent visitor to the restoration work. The summer draws to a close and Tom realises how much his work and companions and the peaceful surroundings have meant to him. In later life he recalls this small but significant interlude in his life, aching for it to return but knowing that it has gone forever.

Graham Swift's *Mothering Sunday* is a very good example of the power of the short novel or novella in the hands of a skilful and experienced writer. It's 30th March 1924, Mothering Sunday, the day when traditionally servants were allowed time off to visit their mothers. But Jane Fairchild, housemaid to the Niven family, is an orphan and neither she nor her employer know what she'll do with her day of freedom. Then the phone rings and the day's events are set in motion.

The narrative grips us from the start, for it's clear that the day will not end happily. We're kept guessing as to the outcome of events and, when tragedy strikes, we're still not clear as to what precisely happens. It's a compelling and teasingly sensual story told in immaculate prose, with not a word out of place. The characters aren't fully developed – the book is too short for that – but they manage to be both representative and unique, true to type and yet interestingly distinctive. The conversation is spare, almost perfunctory, but loaded with meaning. Then there's the added dimension of Jane's reflections which reveal her developing understanding of people and their behaviour, a very important factor later in her life. There's so much to savour in this book and numerous levels of understanding to enjoy in subsequent readings.

Every norm has its exceptions and Steinbeck's *Cannery Row* must rank as a good example, for it conforms to few of the features commonly associated with the short novel. Steinbeck describes his book at the outset: it's about a place and all the people who live there. The sardine canneries built of corrugated iron, the derelict buildings inhabited by down-and-outs, the restaurants, the crowded grocery shops, the laboratories and flophouses are all vividly brought to life. The place is teeming with people – attractive, flawed, complex – so that we really do feel that all life is here. Many of those we meet are on the fringes of society – the idle, the drunkards, the lawbreakers, whores, conmen, the rejected – but Steinbeck presents them non-judgementally and shows us their essential humanity. They have a friendliness and generosity that, in retrospect, may well seem sentimental, but to which we warm instinctively when we're actually reading the book. Steinbeck invites us to accept people as they are, with all their complexity and mixture of good and bad. Cannery Row is a 'dream', a picture of how life can be when people cohere as a community, recognising each other's worth and needs, working for the common good.

The book is full of admirable characters, people with qualities to admire and respect – Lee Chong, the courteous grocer who 'speaks a stately English without ever using the middle R', the grand but kind-hearted Dora Flood who runs the whore house, and the hero of the novel, the wise and serene Doc, whose essential goodness is recognised by everyone. These characters are all based closely on real people for whom Steinbeck felt a great affection and nostalgia. The real-life 'Doc' was Ed Ricketts, a marine biologist who was Steinbeck's closest friend for many years and to whom the book is dedicated. The tidal pool from which Ricketts collects his marine animals is a microcosm of the animal world where creatures interact with their environment – just as *Cannery Row* is a microcosm of the world and its human inhabitants.

One of the most consistently successful British writers of short novels is Penelope Lively, an Oxford history graduate whose *Moon Tiger* won the Booker Prize in 1987 and was one of five novels short-listed in 2018 for the Golden Man Booker award, the outstanding prize-winner in the 50 years of the award's existence. I first discovered Penelope Lively's books in the 1970s when she was gaining a considerable reputation as a children's writer. Daughter Rachel and I shared an enjoyment of her stories. I recently came across one that we read and discussed together when she was 13 or 14 – *Going Back,* a gentle and evocative story of a brother and sister growing up during the years of the Second World War. In middle-age, Jane returns to her childhood home on a Somerset farm and is transported back to a blissfully happy stage in her life. As she contemplates that time, her childhood years merge into a single idyllic picture (tinged with a hint of Dylan Thomas's *Under Milk Wood*):

> "All summers are one haymaking and raspberry time and lanes tented over with leaves and the tipping hillsides bleached pale where they have cut the corn."

1977 saw the publication of Penelope Lively's first adult novel, *The Road to Lichfield.* It heralded a second stage in her career that has been every bit as successful as the first. She is one of many novelists whose early works win acclaim and literary awards, only for their later and more mature works to be somewhat taken for granted. Penelope Lively is in fact a thoughtful and highly creative writer who has constantly grown in stature as she's honed and perfected her skills. *Consequences* and *Family Album,* both written when she was in her mid-seventies, are, for me, particularly fine examples of an author at the height of her powers.

I knew how much my daughter had enjoyed Penelope Lively's stories as a young teenager, but had not until recently fully realised just how influential they'd been in her life. I'd asked her for an off-the-cuff assessment of Lively as a children's writer and received the following email:

"It was Penelope Lively who really helped me to make the transition from childhood fantasy and adventure (Enid Blyton etc.) to adult modern literature. I was very aware as I read her novels that they were more sophisticated, well-crafted and maturely written than the books that I'd read before that point. And nothing after seemed to be a step up in terms of challenge.

I remember enjoying her books so much that, once I'd finished one, I was excited to get down to the library to borrow another. I remember each one individually in a way in which I recall the plot, themes and scenes of few books that I've read since.

When I finally saw the House in Oxford's Norham Gardens for myself the memories of the book flooded back.

Lively's children's novels are among the most precious of my childhood possessions. I have kept them all, while throwing out most of my childhood books in various culls over the years.

I loved the way that historical characters featured large in Lively's books, in an almost ghostly fashion. She evoked historical contexts so powerfully and ignited in me a lifelong interest in the past which led me to study history to degree level."

Penelope Lively's keen interest in memory and the role of the past in people's lives has been maintained throughout her long writing career and is a thread running through both her children's books and her adult novels. Each novel is different in its exploration of the sadness, joy and unpredictability of the human situation, but memories of the past always feature in some way. Penelope Lively moves easily through the different stages of her characters' lives, exploring the many facets of memory – how it works and the tricks it plays, the difficulty of re-constructing past events and the alternative perceptions different people have of the same situation. Key themes are the complex relationship between past, present and future; the changes wrought by time on places, people and society; the power of buildings and artefacts to arouse emotional recollections of bygone times and past lives; and the ties of kinship that help to define who we are.

Shortly after Lively began writing for adults, *Going Back* underwent an interesting metamorphosis: originally written for the 11-14 age group, it was re-issued as an adult novel. The author explains that she'd genuinely thought the novel was a children's book but that

> "...reading it now, I see that it is only tenuously so; the pitch, the voice, the focus are not really those of a true children's book. Looking at it fifteen years later, I see it quite differently, and recognise it as a trial run for preoccupations with the nature of memory, with a certain kind of writing, with economy and allusion. I was flexing muscles, I think, trying things out, and it was only by accident that the result seemed to me and to others to be a book primarily for children."

Opinions vary greatly on the precise difference between children's and adult literature and where the two meet. *Going Back* combines a story about childhood with adult themes. Whether you regard it as primarily a child's or adult's book depends, I suppose, on whether you think its main focus is on the children's reactions to their situation or on the adult's interpretation of past events.

Most novels that combine children's and adults' perceptions of the world provide an effective bridge for teenagers to become adult readers. I'm thinking, for example, of John Boyne's Holocaust novel *The Boy in the Striped Pyjamas* and Mark Haddon's *The Curious Incident of the Dog in the Night-Time*, featuring a young mathematician who has some peculiar behavioural problems, not defined, but seemingly on the autism spectrum. I read these books as adult novels, but I fully appreciate why they have proved so successful with teenagers. Their authors capture the child's view of adult behaviour and Boyne's Bruno and Haddon's Christopher are completely convincing in the ways in which they respond to the unusual situations that they experience.

Both Mark Haddon and John Boyne have demonstrated their serious interest in increasing the number of people who experience the pleasure of reading. *The Curious Incident of the Dog in the Night-Time* was originally published simultaneously in separate editions for children and adults. John Boyne is one of a number of successful novelists who have contributed to the Quick Reads project, an interesting initiative designed to encourage adults who do not often read, or who find reading difficult, to discover the pleasure of books. They are all about 100 pages in length and over 60 titles have been published, three million copies sold and two million loaned by libraries. In a survey covering 50,000 new readers, 98% said that Quick Reads had made a positive impact on their lives. If John Boyne's *The Dare* is representative, the series is also eminently suitable for teenagers who have lost or never acquired the reading habit.

The Dare has a good story-line about a 13-year-old boy, Danny, who encounters a succession of challenging situations arising from his mother's having knocked down a young boy in a driving accident. The injured boy is in a coma in hospital and Danny's mother shuts herself off, full of guilt, leaving her husband and Danny to cope with the events set in train by the accident. The vocabulary and sentence structure are straightforward, but not patronising.

Length of reading material is an important issue in any attempt to encourage non-readers to read for pleasure. It's also a factor in whether or not people maintain the reading habit during periods of pressure and competing demands on their time. The secondary school stage is interesting in this respect. Many children read avidly in the primary school and are happy to move outside their comfort zone in search of new reading experiences. Invariably they become both less frequent and less adventurous in their reading in the secondary school. By the GCSE and A level stages of education many young people, particularly boys, appear to have lost the reading habit altogether.

The teenage years are tightly packed with new interests, opportunities, relationships and challenges, all coinciding with an energy-draining growth spurt. There is a strong case for giving teenagers more space and time to develop their own interests, aptitudes and aspirations. Instead, we pile on the pressure with a highly prescriptive and demanding study workload that spills over into their own time with ever-increasing homework assignments.

One option available to those who have a problem finding time for reading for pleasure is the short story, and many novelists experiment with this form of fiction, some with great success. The novella and the long family saga are simply variations of the novel, but the short story is a distinctive craft form in its own right and presents a writer with a different, if related, set of challenges. Designed to be read at one sitting, it's most typically about 10-25 pages in length. As with the very short novel, the writer focuses on a single incident or closely related incidents, but there's no space to analyse the situation in detail or to develop either the narrative or the characters to any great extent. Readers sometimes have to pick up the thread of the story part-way through a sequence of events and to work out some of the implications for themselves. The interaction of character and event is a very simplified version of the kind of complex plot we have in a novel. Instead of a plot, the short story usually seeks to create a mood that produces a single emotional reaction.

The short story has a long history as a genre, having been a powerful means of communication for centuries. It is the most natural form of narrative and the way in which children first experience the joy of reading and listening to fiction. I first stumbled on adult short stories via a huge collection of Guy de Maupassant's works in translation, unearthed in my Singapore bookshop. The name meant nothing to me and it was years later that I became aware of the Frenchman's reputation and the influence of his iconic *La Parure* (*The Necklace*) which made such an impression on me when I first read it.

The Necklace tells the sad story of Madame Matilde Loisel, a young woman much frustrated by her lower middle class status. Her husband, a lowly clerk in the Ministry of Education, tries to accommodate his wife's desire for a better style of life and manages to obtain tickets for an office party. Mathilde refuses to go, as she has nothing appropriate to wear. Her husband uses his limited savings to buy her a dress, but there is then a problem over what to wear with it. Declining her husband's suggestions of a spray of flowers, she asks a well-off friend if she might borrow a piece of her jewellery. The friend responds generously, allowing her to choose a large diamond necklace from her collection. Mathilde's evening is a huge success and gives her a taste of the lifestyle she so desires. But, when she and her husband return home, the necklace is missing. All efforts to find it come to nothing and the young couple decide they must conceal what has happened and find a replacement. The cost of a replica is prohibitive: Mathilde and her husband are forced to sell all their belongings and take out loans at high rates of interest. Years pass and one day Mathilde encounters her old friend, with whom she's long lost contact. Her friend doesn't recognise her – she's aged greatly and is dressed very poorly. On impulse, Mathilde decides to recount the whole story of the lost and replaced necklace. Her friend is deeply moved and takes both her hands: "Oh! my poor Mathilde! But mine was only paste, not worth more than 500 francs at most!"

The key elements of this Maupassant story are very clearly narrated: Mathilde's obsessive desire for a wealthy lifestyle, her frustration at her husband's limited means of satisfying her dream, her lack of restraint in response to her friend's generosity in letting her choose the best piece from her jewellery box, Mathilde's intense enjoyment of the party, the crippling cost of replacing the lost necklace. It's extremely economical story-telling pruned to the bare essentials. We know nothing about the young couple's lives and have only a hint or two concerning their characters.

Everything in this story hinges on its ironies: the contrast between Mathilde's aspirations and her reduced circumstances, her choice of the best item of jewellery which makes its loss more serious, and, most importantly, the awful consequences of the couple's desire not to lose face by admitting to having lost the necklace. I don't think we actually empathise with Mathilde – we don't know her sufficiently for that – but we are strongly affected by the situation. The 'twist-in-the end' is one of the hallmarks of Maupassant's story-telling and *The Necklace* is the most frequently-quoted example.

Not all short stories are as neatly constructed and powerfully concluded as Maupassant's. In fact some end quite abruptly or just tail away rather unsatisfactorily. A short story either works for me or it doesn't. It's not really substantial enough to be successful in some respects and not in others, which is often how I feel about a novel. I think I expect too much from short stories: by their very nature they're never going to be as absorbing as a novel. You don't get to know the characters well enough to identify with them as fully as you do even in a short novel and, if you do begin to find them interesting, then the speedy termination of a short story can be frustrating. It's not easy for writers to get the balance right.

William Boyd, accomplished novelist and short story writer, believes that, in capturing the essence of a specific human situation, the short story meets a basic need, something very deep in our nature. I don't know whether that's true but, despite my reservations concerning this particular form of fiction, I do find myself quite frequently drawn to volumes of short stories – especially if they've been written by a novelist whom I admire. I've just finished, and greatly enjoyed, William Trevor's *Last Stories*, published two years after his death in 2016.

Writers are habitual observers and listeners, and many of the people they watch and overhear find their way into their books and plays. Harold Pinter and Joseph Conrad were prime examples. William Trevor was another. His long-term literary agent tells how Trevor would sit on park benches and listen to people's conversations. Apparently he never wanted to listen to the whole story, but would get up and move on as soon as he had heard the small amount that he needed to trigger his imagination. This insight into the source of the author's ideas helps to explain the feeling we have in reading a Trevor short story that we are eavesdroppers, listening in to the most personal details of ordinary people's lives which are being revealed, often for the first time.

As with Trevor's novels, his ten *Last Stories* cover a wide range of human situations, but they are variations on a number of familiar Trevor themes – in particular, loss, loneliness and the failure to connect. They are sad stories of people who have missed out on the good things in life or who, having experienced them, have had them snatched away from them. There are casualties of broken love relationships and friendships, widows and widowers, people who endure loveless marriages or walk away from them, or are themselves abandoned by their partner. Some of the central characters are resigned to their loneliness and heartache; others seek a remedy, sometimes obsessively, so that their behaviour becomes eccentric and detached from reality. The narratives usually involve three or four characters, some of them key players, whilst others get drawn in accidentally, and sometimes reluctantly. They include characters who are tempted to exploit other people's misfortunes, but also those who develop a compassion for a stranger's unhappiness in a way that restores our faith in human nature.

William Trevor is a consummate craftsman, a sophisticated and skilful story-teller. His irony is subtler than Maupassant's and he builds tension more gradually and gently. We think we can see where the narrative is going, but are frequently hoodwinked into anticipating a neatly contrived climax that doesn't materialise. There is an enigmatic quality to some of the stories, some mystery surrounding a character that we expect to have clarified, but which remains vague and uncertain. One of the lessons that several of Trevor's characters learn about their situation is that there aren't clear explanations for what happens to us, or satisfactory answers to all of life's problems. Sometimes we just have to accept that life is a messy business and stop looking for a meaning in every twist and turn that we experience.

Choose any one of the *Last Stories* for an indication of the distinctive flavour of William Trevor's story-telling, but read them all to appreciate their variety. The simplest and shortest story is *The Piano Tutor's Pupil* about a strange boy who is both musical genius and kleptomaniac. *Mrs Crasthorpe* is more complex, causing the reader to change perceptions and sympathies as the narrative unfolds and the three main characters are seen in different situations. *An Idyll in Winter* is quite different again: a delightful, but eventually painful, love story that illustrates the power of the past to determine events in the present.

Short stories are normally written by authors best known for their novels, but occasionally writers are recognised as much for their short-story writing as for their full-length fiction. Very rarely does an author concentrate solely on short stories. Alice Munro breaks the mould spectacularly: she has produced 14 collections of short stories over a writing career spanning nearly fifty years – but no novels.

Alice Munro knew from an early age that she wanted to write and, as a young married woman with a family, she chose short stories as her medium. She said she didn't have the time to write a novel. Her collections of stories made an immediate impact on both the critics and general public and she accrued awards throughout her long career, culminating in the Nobel Prize in Literature in 2013 for her lifelong achievement as 'master of the short story'. She did try to write a novel, but, urged by her publisher to keep to the short story, she decided she had 'to recognise her limitations'.

There is an irony here, as Alice Munro probably goes further than any other modern writer of short stories in endowing her stories with the emotional depth and intensity of a novel. She often defies the conventions and restrictions of short-story writing – in the way in which she develops her characters, builds up suspense, and moves backwards and forwards in time. She is a great polisher, revising and re-writing her stories, even after publication. She works hard at the endings to ensure that they're an intrinsic part of the whole story.

Alice Munro was born in Huron County in South-Western Ontario and there is a strong regional focus to her stories. She writes about ordinary people in rural areas – their trials and tribulations, the paradoxes and ambiguities of their lives, the key turning points and revelations that help her characters make sense of particular events. A recurring theme is the frustration her characters experience as a result of deep-rooted customs and traditions. My most recent Munro acquisition is *Too Much Happiness,* written in 2013 when the author was 79. It's a collection of powerful and dramatic stories in which the characters face some very challenging and difficult situations.

Not the least of the demands that story-telling makes on authors is for them to keep coming up with new insights into different facets of the human situation. Neither Alice Munro nor William Trevor seems to have any difficulty in this respect. The Complete Short Stories of either of these writers would be a good book choice for guests on Desert Island Discs.

10.

The Ultimate Achievement

You don't have to have a degree in agriculture to take delight in a lovely garden, or to have attended the Slade School of Fine Art in order to appreciate a Constable or Monet. Nor is studying literature a pre-requisite for enjoying a good novel. Many children learn to enjoy stories at a very early age and some will have begun a love affair with the novel well before they are required to study Eng. Lit. for GCSE. Authors are naturally pleased at the effect on sales if their books are chosen as set texts for GCSE and A level courses, but they often express concern at the classroom process of analysis and criticism which, as we all know, can alienate the very people it's designed to enthuse.

The study of literature provides a useful academic language with which to discuss writers' skills and works. But increased awareness of the writing process comes at a cost. A book is a live thing with the potential to inform and educate, to entertain, or to move a reader to tears or laughter. It's not a dead animal on a slab waiting to be dissected in the biology lab. When reading a novel, you don't want to be sidetracked into identifying and analysing aspects of the author's style. A good author is well aware of this and tries to ensure that the methods used to arouse and maintain the reader's interest are as unobtrusive as possible.

The 2018 centenary of Leonard Bernstein's birth was celebrated with special concerts all over the world. A TV panel of instrumentalists and singers discussed his music before an Albert Hall prom that featured his work: they agreed that one of his distinctive attributes as a composer was his ability to communicate directly to an audience, without his technique getting in the way. I appreciate that quality in any creative artist, but especially in a writer. I'm impressed by authors who keep in the background and are able to generate a powerful story without raising their voice or heightening their language – authors who draw us into their novels easily and naturally by the depth of their perception and the fluency of their writing.

Many early novels opened with a lengthy introduction to the characters and the place in which they lived. In a more frenetic age the novelist usually seeks to grab the reader's attention immediately and to feed in any necessary background information later. Consequently, the modern novel often begins with high drama on the front page. David Guterson's highly-acclaimed *Snow Falling on Cedars* opens in the courtroom with a murder trial, J M Coetzee's 1999 Booker-prize-winning novel, *Disgrace*, begins with a sex scene in a brothel, and the first page of Richard Hughes' *The Fox in the Attic* describes two men crossing a sea-marsh, one of whom has the body of a dead child slung over his shoulder. But it's possible to arouse interest in much less and obvious ways. Here's the opening to Colm Toibin's *Brooklyn*:

"Eilis Lacey, sitting at the window of the upstairs living room in the house of Friary Street, noticed her sister walking briskly from work. She watched Rose crossing the street from sunlight into shade, carrying the new leather handbag that she had bought in Clery's in Dublin in the sale. Rose was wearing a cream-coloured cardigan over her shoulders. Her golf-clubs were in the hall; in a few minutes, Eilis knew, someone would call for her and her sister would not return until the summer evening had faded."

Spare, gentle, quiet, this is trademark Toibin – the simplest of domestic scenes in which the reader views one character through the eyes of another. The sentence structure is very uncomplicated, the words almost entirely of one or two syllables. The author leaves the reader to interpret the situation with just a hint or two at the significance of what we're being told. We can learn a good deal about an author's strengths from the opening sentences of a novel, which I suppose is the reason that bookshop-browsers often read the first page or two of a novel that looks interesting. The best test of an author's quality, however, is how well the big scenes, set pieces and dramatic events are handled. Do they make an impact on us without our being aware how hard the writer is working to produce the desired effect?

I've just read Graham Swift's *Ever After* for the umpteenth time. It's an emotionally and intellectually stimulating novel that explores a number of Swift's favourite themes – the way in which our lives are shaped by the past, and by circumstances beyond our control, and how our understanding of life is flawed and our memories of the past distorted. Death, suicide, loss, bereavement all feature prominently, but it's by no means a melancholy book: both the main characters experience intense happiness in their marriages. The courtship of Ruth by Bill Unwin is a delightful love story and their anticipation of their first night together is particularly poignant. The description of that night, with all its emotion, excitement and intimacy, is an excellent example of a writer's knowing just how much to tell and how much to leave to the reader's imagination. Graham Swift not only takes me inside his characters, so that I share their pains and pleasures, but he moves me to a deep sadness for the human condition and its implications for me personally and those dear to me. *Ever After* is a complex novel, but very clear in its vision and told in admirably uncluttered and unpretentious prose.

It's difficult to say precisely what prompts someone to read a book several times when there are so many promising new titles coming onto the market. I sometimes go back over parts of a novel that I've read in order to clarify something that's puzzling me or to check on an early event which proved more significant as the story unfolded, but I don't recall going through a whole book again because parts were obscure or ambiguous. However, I've occasionally been tempted to re-read a densely-packed novel because I've felt there had been too much to absorb at a first reading. But a desire to read a book more than twice? What's going on there? Obviously there's a strong sense of rapport with the author, but also something very special that makes a particular novel stand out from the rest of a writer's works and become one of the reader's really memorable experiences.

Many novels keep the reader guessing about the direction and outcome of the plot, building up suspense by releasing information gradually, introducing new and unexpected possibilities, teasing the reader with red herrings and false trails. With a knowledge of the outcomes, the element of surprise isn't, of course, there in second and subsequent readings. But in some books this doesn't seem to matter unduly. There's an enigmatic heroine in Bernhard Schlink's *The Reader* whose secrecy about her past life arouses keen interest and builds gradually to a totally unexpected revelation towards the end of the book. Yet the novel is powerful on so many fronts that I found foreknowledge of the mystery no deterrent to reading it several times. It's a book that simply ticks all the boxes.

Emotionally harrowing, philosophically profound, *The Reader* poses fundamental questions about human nature and behaviour, questions that we habitually avoid confronting. It's a beautifully balanced and structured novel – in the blend of narrative, plot and theme, in the contrasting nature and background of Michael and Hanna, in the fine dilemmas that these characters face, and in the conflicting emotions that the reader experiences in empathising with them. The style is direct, crystal clear and elegant, an illustration of the power of simple words ordered to perfection. There's a wholeness and completeness to this book, an artistic integrity that made me want my first reading of it to be at a single sitting. I imagine the sexual content and the fact that it's written by a German will ensure that *The Reader* never finds its way onto an English literature examination syllabus. Let's hope so. This is not a book to be hung and quartered for the gratification of academics. It's a book to be read and enjoyed. And then read again.

One of the features of a novel that distinguishes it from other linguistic art forms is its intimacy – the way it draws readers into the writer's imaginary world and takes them right inside the hearts and minds of the characters. A significant focus in *The Reader* is the moral dilemma experienced by Michael, the main male character, after he discovers Hanna's secret. The reader shares every twist and turn of his agonising as he thinks of ways forward and then changes his mind. In a play or film there's no effective way of dealing with situations like this and the screen version of *The Reader* doesn't attempt to do so. Stage plays and films tend to concentrate on the action and to heighten the dramatic impact of the big scenes. They also, of course, make use of a wide range of technical aids – sound effects, lights, props, background music, choreography.

Another example is Michael Cunningham's *The Hours*, a subtle interweaving of the stories of three women who lived at different times in the 20th century. Virginia Woolf, Clarissa Vaughan and Laura Brown are all exceptional women with highly developed sensitivities, capable of an intense appreciation of life's finer moments, but also fragile and vulnerable. The comparisons between the three characters and the themes that connect their separate existences make for fascinating reading.

Stephen Daldry's screen adaptation of Cunningham's novel features Nicole Kidman (Virginia Woolf), Julianne Moore (Laura Brown) and Meryl Streep, a big favourite of mine, as Clarissa Vaughan. It had a mixed reception from the critics, but it's a lovely film, with powerful performances by all three actresses and a very good supporting cast. The screen version is largely faithful to the book, yet the film and novel are very different. It's not possible in a film to convey the feelings and thoughts of the three main characters that form the major part of the novel. Instead, key incidents are made more dramatic to increase the tension and conflicting emotions that the characters feel. For example, in the film Laura Brown is portrayed as more suicidal than she is in the book, her lips-to-lips kissing with another woman is more passionate and suggestive, a drive to a hotel becomes manic and dangerous, her delay in getting to see someone on his birthday causes her to be tearful. The effect of these changes is to make the conflicts in the film much less subtle and complex than in the book, where they tend to stay beneath the surface. This is not a criticism of the film, simply an indication of the distinguishing features of different art forms. A novel and a film can tell the same story, but they will always do so in different ways.

Writers are naturally keen to make the most of the big scenes and dramatic moments in their novels and this often leads to a heightening of the language and imagery at key points of the narrative. On occasions, novelists are tempted to introduce devices akin to the film director's techniques – to quicken the pace of the narrative with a succession of short urgent sentences, to introduce a strong beat or staccato rhythm, to adopt a disjointed or fractured prose style that mirrors a sense of disorder or confusion in the story. This sort of thing sometimes works, but it can easily be a distraction. Experienced writers are usually sparing in their use of literary tricks and devices, preferring to allow the dramatic situations to unravel without stage directions. The more powerful and dramatic a novel is, the less need there is for any embellishment. Lightness of touch, restraint, a willingness to allow readers space for their own thoughts, emotions and interpretations – these are admirable qualities in a writer.

One of a poet's aims is to enrich our lives by revealing to us the remarkable things that surround us all the time of which we are unaware. Some novelists seek to do the same. One of the characters in Jon McGregor's first book, *If Nobody Speaks of Remarkable Things,* entreats his young daughter to be observant of everything around her: "this is a very big world and there are many, many things you could miss if you are not careful.... there are remarkable things all the time, right in front of us", but, he says, our eyes are dimmed in the way that clouds obscure the sun and our lives are paler and poorer because we do not see things for what they are.

When previously unknown writers appear on the literary scene they are often heralded as 'a new voice'. The term was certainly valid when the 26-year-old Jon McGregor produced *If Nobody Speaks of Remarkable Things* in 2002. McGregor brought an exciting new dimension to the modern novel, speaking directly to the reader in a fresh and powerful way. His early promise has been fully realised, both as a novelist and short story writer. His 2017 novel, *Reservoir 13,* tells the story of a close-knit Derbyshire community shaken by a tragedy that remains in people's minds for many years. This key event provides the novel's dramatic focal point, but McGregor's main interest lies in the lives of the ordinary people who make up the rural community he describes. We meet some 50 or 60 characters, a few brush strokes at a time, the focus constantly changing from one group or situation to another. We follow the characters' fluctuating fortunes as time passes, the twists and turns of their relationships, their response to changing circumstances and expectations – all played out against the changing seasons and annual community events. We are given a clear picture of the village setting, whilst the natural world is vividly portrayed with a constant commentary on the ever-changing plant and animal life in the surrounding countryside.

Jon McGregor's descriptions are delightful – short, precise and seemingly effortless:

> "At the allotment the last of the leeks were yellow against the snow, fat-bodied and toppling , their papery skins peeling away."

> "In the conifer plantation the goldcrest nests were thickly-packed with eggs the size of babies' thumbs."

The impact stems from the simplicity and accuracy of the detail. Sometimes the background pictures are no more than brief reminders of a seasonal detail to which we have already been introduced, or a plain statement of fact to remind us of the backcloth to the narrative. There is often an appeal to the ear as well as the eye.

McGregor has a poet's or artist's interest in everything around him. He builds up a panorama of what appear to be casual pictures and sensations that give the places, characters and situations a strong physical presence. He is adept at capturing a poignant scene, an amusing incident, a fleeting expression or meaningful intonation:

> "She noticed how still Mr Wilson was beside her. He felt poised. They were sitting closer together than she'd realised and now he lifted a hand from his lap and laid it on her knee. Somewhere a little higher than her knee. It rested there, loosely, and they both looked at it. For a moment they seemed as surprised as each other. She lifted his hand,

which was softer and warmer to the touch than she might
have imagined, and placed it gently back on his lap."

McGregor is particularly skilful at conveying a mood and
hinting at the undercurrents below the surface of a seemingly
simple scene. Among the many characters in *Reservoir 13* there
are four youngsters whom we follow through their teenage
years, and, as the novel develops, we share an evening with
them at their favourite drinking place before they all go off to
their different universities. It's an evening of mixed emotions.
They are good friends and openly admit that they'll miss each
other: they promise to keep in touch. At the same time there's
a sense of anticipation as they contemplate new experiences
ahead. Two of the group, Lynsey and James, are in a
relationship and have had a somewhat confusing conversation
in which they have agreed that they don't want to break up,
but would like to feel free to go out with other people and then
see how they feel at Christmas or in the following summer.
There is a slight edginess on Lynsey's part.

The occasion begins to hang heavily over the group and
Lynsey, who has a car, says she'll get going. First, though,
James leads them through a ritual that they've established over
the years – a barefooted scamper to a shallow stretch of river
where they paddle up to their shins, shrieking and protesting
at the coldness of the water. Then the slamming of car doors
and Lynsey swinging her car out of the carpark, the headlights
spotlighting the friends' empty glasses and catching a curling
wisp of smoke from a dying cigarette in an ashtray. The
evening is over and with it a stage in the characters' lives and
relationships. Such a simple and ordinary scene, but a moving
reminder of the passing of time and transitoriness of each

period of our lives. It typifies the author's undemonstrative storytelling.

Novelists who engage our minds and feelings without striving for our attention or for dramatic effect provide a refreshing alternative to the relentless hype that accompanies so much of what we read and listen to in our daily lives. What greater relief from the advertisers, public relations agents and spin doctors than a novel that gives the reader space and time to think about the issues that it raises, without intervention from the author? What better antidote to the sensationalism and trivia of so much of what passes for entertainment on TV with its frenetic and falsely jocular presenters, contrived audience euphoria, canned laughter and 'strong language'?

We live in a time of unprecedented manipulation of the truth that has destroyed the conventional distinction between 'fact' and fiction'. Every attempt to obtain reliable information, to separate the real from the illusory, to get to the truth of a situation is systematically undermined by misinformation and 'fake news'. Deception and indoctrination are big business: millions of pounds are spent in persuading the masses to think and behave in particular ways. The web has given corrupt businesses, fanatics, perverts and extremists of all kinds a ready means of exploiting the young, the elderly and other vulnerable members of society. Social media encourages us to cheat on our partner, to become a member of the National Front or ISIS, to commit suicide. There is a strong vested interest in undermining the rule of law and destabilising society. At the press of a button you can access detailed guidance on how to cheat in exams, to submit a fraudulent claim to an insurance company, to make a bomb to kill and maim innocent people.

There is widespread distrust of politicians, the police and legal system, big business and the banks.

We have created a state of contradiction and confusion in which the world of fact has become a fiction. Increasingly, I find myself looking to literature for confirmation of the fundamental truths that have become obscured in real life. In a 2017 interview, Richard Flanagan, author of *The Narrow Road to the Deep North,* winner of the 2014 Man Booker Prize, made the following comment on the modern novelist's search for truth:

> "Fiction is not a lie, but a truth, a fundamental and necessary truth, that we need as much as we need food or sex. Without fiction we poison ourselves on the lies of the first person."

Early novels, such as *Moll Flanders, Tom Jones* and *Pamela,* were fictional biographies. Since that time the novel has become steadily more complex and sophisticated. Authors are now multi-taskers, seeking to satisfy their readers' wide-ranging expectations – for a pacy narrative, distinctive characters, realistic plot, tense drama, a strong sense of time and place, new perspectives on age-old human truths. However, of all its component parts, the defining feature of the modern novel is the author's view of the human situation – the ideas and observations that engage our hearts and minds and enhance our understanding of our daily lives and our complex world.

Acknowledgements

I should like to thank

– my wife, Jill; daughters, Rachel and Sarah; and regular correspondent, David Woods, for their invaluable support and critical readings of the draft copy of my book;

– all who have discussed this book with me and offered pertinent advice: Tony and Lesley Lewis, Mariella Wilson, John Sherrington, Catherine Randall, Chris Wiltshire, Joan Cole, Tony Barr and Alex Batho;

– everyone who has written or spoken to me about their childhood experiences of reading for pleasure;

– family and friends for sharing their love of books with me;

– Fern Bushnell and the rest of the Troubador team for their constant encouragement and advice: it's been a pleasure working with them.

Index of Authors and Novels